Deep Brain Reorienting for Beginners

A Plain Language Introduction to DBR, the Brainstem, and the Neuroscience of Shock, Attachment, and Trauma Wounding

Rudolph Alfred Boyd

Disclaimer

This book is for general education and information only. It explains what Deep Brain Reorienting is and how it is meant to work. It does not teach you to perform Deep Brain Reorienting on yourself or on anyone else. Deep Brain Reorienting is a clinical method delivered by trained mental health professionals. Reading about it is not the same as receiving it, and this book is not a substitute for assessment, diagnosis, or treatment by a qualified clinician.

Deep Brain Reorienting and DBR are terms associated with the clinical work of Dr. Frank Corrigan and his colleagues, and may be claimed as trademarks of their respective owners. They are used in this book in a descriptive, editorial sense, to identify and discuss the therapy, and no affiliation, sponsorship, or endorsement is implied. This book is an independent introduction written for general readers. It is not affiliated with, authorized by, or endorsed by Dr. Corrigan, his co authors, or any organization that trains or certifies practitioners in Deep Brain Reorienting. The people described in these pages are composites, built from common patterns rather than real named individuals, with identifying details changed.

Nothing here is medical or psychological advice for your particular situation. This book is provided without warranty of any kind, and the author assumes no liability for any outcome arising from its use. If you are living with the effects of trauma, or if any part of this book stirs up distress, please reach out to a licensed professional or a local crisis service. The research described here was accurate to the best of the author's knowledge at the time of writing. Science moves, so check current sources for the latest findings.

First edition, 2026

ISBN: 979-8-90599-851-5

Table of Contents

Preface

Deep Brain Reorienting has moved, in a short time, from a small clinical innovation to a subject discussed in trauma trainings, professional podcasts, and therapy rooms across several countries. The research is early but active, with a first randomized controlled trial published in 2023 and a full clinical text released in 2024. What has not kept pace is accessible explanation. For a reader who is not a clinician, the available writing can be difficult to enter, and the result is a widening gap between how often the approach is mentioned and how well it is understood.

Deep Brain Reorienting, usually shortened to DBR, is a psychotherapy developed by the psychiatrist Frank Corrigan. It works with structures deep in the brainstem and midbrain that respond to threat in the first fraction of a second, before conscious emotion forms. Its central proposal is that certain trauma is held in this early, pre-emotional layer, and that healing can reach it by returning gently to the physical orienting response that began the reaction. This is what sets DBR apart from approaches that work mainly with memories, thoughts, or emotions: it starts earlier, at the shock beneath the feeling.

The difficulty for most people is not a shortage of interest but a shortage of clear information. Someone who hears that DBR helped a friend, or who reads that it targets the brainstem, has few places to turn for an explanation that does not assume a background in neuroscience. The available accounts are written for practitioners, and the newcomer is left with terms rather than understanding.

This book closes that gap. It is a plain-language introduction that follows a single, consistent line: it explains the deep-brain science in ordinary words, shows what a DBR session involves, sets the approach beside other trauma therapies such as EMDR and

Brainspotting, examines what the current evidence does and does not establish, and describes how to find qualified help. The aim is a reader who finishes able to explain DBR clearly and make an informed decision about it.

It is written first for curious newcomers and for people affected by trauma who want to understand a further option. Clinicians and students new to DBR will also find it a useful orientation before they turn to specialist sources.

A clear statement of limits belongs here. This book explains the approach; it does not teach anyone to practice it, and it is not a manual for self-treatment. DBR is delivered by trained professionals, and reading about it is not the same as receiving it. The evidence remains early, so the book presents DBR as a promising development rather than an established cure, and nothing in it is a substitute for care from a qualified clinician. What it offers instead is understanding: a clear, honest, and welcoming first map of Deep Brain Reorienting.

Chapter 1.0: Introduction

Elena had done the work. Six years of therapy, two different trauma programs, a stack of books on her nightstand tall enough to prop up a laptop. She could explain her childhood better than most people can explain their commute. She knew her triggers. She had language for all of it.

And then her manager cleared his throat in a certain way during a meeting, and she was gone. Not gone from the room. Gone somewhere older and smaller, heart hammering, face hot, a feeling of dread arriving a full second before any thought did. By the time she could name what was happening, it had already happened. Again.

That night she sat in her car in the office parking lot and asked the question that a lot of people ask after years of good, honest effort. What is wrong with me that this still happens? She had insight. She had tools. She had a therapist she trusted. So why did her body keep reacting a full beat before her mind had any chance to catch up?

Here is what nobody had told Elena yet. The problem was probably not that she needed more insight. The problem was that all her good work had been aimed at the part of the reaction that comes second. There is a part that comes first. It is faster than thought, faster than feeling, and most trauma therapy walks right past it. A newer approach called Deep Brain Reorienting is built to find that first part and work with it directly. This book is about that approach, and about the strange, hopeful idea underneath it.

By the end of this chapter you will know what Deep Brain Reorienting is in plain language, who created it, and why it exists at all. You will understand the basic puzzle it is trying to solve, which is why some people stay stuck even after years of good therapy. You will also get a clear and honest picture of what this book can and cannot do for you, so you are not waiting for it to be something it is not. Think of this chapter as the front porch. We are just getting you in the door and pointing at the rooms.

1.1 The Stuck Person Problem

You have probably met someone like Elena. You might be someone like Elena. Smart, self aware, willing to do hard emotional work, and still ambushed by reactions that seem to come from nowhere and refuse to shrink no matter how much they get talked about.

For a long time, the standard explanation was that these people needed more. More sessions. More insight. More time. Sometimes that is true. But sometimes a person can have all the insight in the world and still get hijacked, and the extra sessions just add more understanding on top of a reaction that was never really about understanding in the first place.

This is the puzzle that trauma specialists have been circling for decades. Talk therapy helps a lot of people. It also leaves a stubborn group stuck, people whose bodies keep reacting as if the past were still happening even though their minds know better. The famous book on this, by a psychiatrist named Bessel van der Kolk, is called *The Body Keeps the Score* (van der Kolk, 2014), and the title alone tells you where the field started looking. Not just the mind. The body. The nervous system. The parts of us that react before we can think.

Deep Brain Reorienting belongs to that search. It starts from a simple hunch. If the reaction fires before thought and before feeling, then maybe healing has to reach that early, too. Maybe you cannot fully calm a reaction by working only on the layer that shows up last.

1.2 What DBR Actually Is

Let's name it plainly. Deep Brain Reorienting, usually shortened to **DBR**, is a form of trauma therapy that works with the oldest, deepest part of the brain, the part that reacts to threat in the first split second before emotions like fear or shame have formed.

It was developed by **Frank Corrigan**, a Scottish psychiatrist who spent more than thirty years treating trauma in Scotland's health service and who kept running into the stuck person problem (Corrigan & Christie-Sands, 2020). He had trained in other trauma methods. He kept asking what earlier layer was being missed. DBR is his answer.

The word *reorienting* is the key to the whole thing. **Orienting** is what your brain does when something grabs your attention. A sound behind you, and your head turns before you decide to turn it. That turn, that instant snap of attention toward a possible threat, is one of the most ancient moves the nervous system has. DBR proposes that in a moment of trauma, especially sudden or shocking trauma, that orienting response gets locked in a certain way, and that you can help it complete and settle by returning to it gently and letting the body find its way through the original sequence (Corrigan & Christie-Sands, 2020).

If that sounds abstract right now, good. It is supposed to. We are going to spend the whole book making it concrete. For this chapter, hold onto just this: DBR works earlier than most therapies, on the reaction that comes before the feeling.

1.3 Example

Meet Marcus. He is a paramedic, mid forties, calm in a crisis in a way that makes other people trust him instantly. He came to therapy not for a single dramatic event but because he had started to feel numb, like he was watching his own life through a slightly dirty window.

In one session his therapist asked about a call from years earlier, a bad one involving a child. Marcus started to describe it in his usual flat, professional voice. He had told the story before. It never moved him. That was part of the problem.

His old approach had been to talk about it clearly and stay in control, which is exactly what his job had trained him to do. It worked for getting through shifts. It did nothing for the numbness, because the talking never touched the part of him that had frozen in the first half second of arriving on that scene.

His therapist, trained in DBR, slowed everything down and asked him to notice not the story but a small tightening at the back of his neck as he pictured the moment before he stepped out of the ambulance. Marcus stayed with that tightening. For a long minute nothing happened. Then his eyes filled, and something in his chest that had been clenched for years quietly let go.

What this means for you: The thing keeping a person stuck is often not the story they can tell. It is a small physical moment they have never gone back to. DBR is built to find that moment.

1.4 Who This Book Is For

This book is for the curious. Maybe you heard DBR mentioned on a podcast and got interested. Maybe you have been through trauma yourself and you are quietly hunting for something that might reach the part nothing else has reached. Maybe you love someone who is stuck and you want to understand their options.

And maybe you are a therapist. A lot of therapists are hearing about DBR right now and want a way in that does not require reading a dense academic book first. You are welcome here too. There is a whole chapter later just for you.

Wherever you are coming from, the promise is the same. You will leave understanding this approach well enough to talk about it, to spot when it might be a good fit, and to decide what you want to do next. You do not need to be an expert. You just need to be willing to take it one step at a time.

1.5 What This Book Will Not Do

Here is the honest part, and it matters. This book will not teach you to do Deep Brain Reorienting. Not on yourself, not on anyone else.

That is not me being cautious for the sake of it. DBR is a clinical method that reaches into raw, pre verbal parts of a person's response to threat. In trained hands, with careful pacing, that is where its power comes from. Without training, poking around in that same territory can stir up more than a person can hold. The people who deliver DBR go through sequential professional training with live practice and supervision before they use it with clients (Kearney et al., 2023). A book cannot replace that, and this one will not pretend to.

You might be thinking, then what is the point of reading it? Fair question. The point is understanding. Understanding helps you choose. It helps you find the right kind of help instead of the first kind. It helps you ask better questions of a therapist. And if you are a clinician, it helps you decide if this is worth your training time and money before you spend either. Understanding is not a consolation prize. It is the thing that lets you take a good next step instead of a random one.

This book also will not oversell. DBR is new. The research is early and promising, not vast and settled. You will get the real picture, including the parts that are still question marks.

1.6 Example

Meet Gemma. She is a licensed counselor with eight years of experience and a waiting list. She is good at her job. She also has three or four clients who have plateaued, and it bothers her the way a splinter bothers you.

She kept seeing DBR mentioned in her professional groups. Every time, she felt a flicker of interest and a heavier wave of tiredness. Another method. Another training. Another weekend and another few hundred dollars to learn something that might turn out to be a repackaged version of what she already does.

What she tried first was the obvious thing. She bought the main academic book on DBR. She got four chapters in, hit a wall of brainstem terminology, and set it on the shelf next to her other good intentions. The book was not bad. It was just not built for a busy clinician trying to decide if this was worth a deeper look.

What worked was starting smaller. She found a plain language overview, read it in an evening, and finally understood the core idea well enough to know it was genuinely different from her current tools. Now she could make a real decision instead of a guilty non decision.

What this means for you: Sometimes the barrier is not your ability. It is the size of the first step. A gentle overview can be the thing that makes a big topic finally click.

1.7 When This Idea Doesn't Land

The most common way this chapter falls flat is that it sounds too good. A hidden first moment, a deeper layer, a fresh kind of hope. If you have been let down by treatments before, that can read as one more shiny promise, and a healthy part of you gets suspicious. Good. Keep that part.

Here is why the suspicion is worth holding onto rather than acting on right away. New trauma methods often arrive with big claims and thin evidence, and some of them fade. DBR is new enough that we genuinely do not know how large its place will be.

What we do know is early and encouraging, and we will look straight at it in a later chapter rather than asking you to take anything on faith.

Three things to try if this chapter left you skeptical or unsettled:

1. Read on to the evidence chapter before you decide what you think. Judge the idea on the data, not on the hope.
2. Notice which reaction is louder in you, the hope or the doubt, and let both ride along. You do not have to resolve them yet.
3. If any of this stirred something personal and heavy, set the book down and talk to someone. Understanding trauma from the outside is calm work. Feeling it is not, and you should not do the second part alone.

If the whole topic feels like too much right now, that is allowed. Put the book away and come back when you are ready. The ideas are patient.

1.8 The Quick Version

Some people do years of honest therapy and still get hijacked by reactions that fire faster than thought. That is the stuck person problem, and it is what Deep Brain Reorienting was built to address.

DBR is a trauma therapy developed by the Scottish psychiatrist Frank Corrigan. It works with the deepest, oldest part of the brain, the part that reacts to threat in the first split second, before fear or shame have formed. Its central move is returning gently to that early orienting moment and letting the body complete a sequence that got locked during the trauma.

This book is a plain language door into that world. It is for anyone curious, including therapists who want a way in without a dense textbook. It will help you understand DBR well enough to talk about it, spot when it fits, and choose a good next step.

It will not teach you to perform DBR, because that takes real training with supervision, and it will not oversell an approach whose evidence is still young. What it offers instead is a clear, honest picture. That picture is enough to make a good decision, which is more than most people start with.

Chapter 2.0: The Shock Before Feeling

Layla was telling her therapist about an ordinary afternoon. Her partner had come home, glanced at the dishes in the sink, and said nothing. Just glanced. Within a second Layla's stomach had dropped and her shoulders had climbed toward her ears, and she spent the rest of the evening braced for a fight that never came.

Her therapist asked a careful question. Not why do you think you reacted, but what happened first, in your body, in the very first instant. Layla stopped. She had never thought about a first instant. The reaction had always felt like one solid thing, like a wall falling on her.

She closed her eyes and went back to the moment. And there it was, so quick she had never caught it before. Before the fear, before the story about being judged, before any of it, there was a tiny jolt. A flinch behind her eyes and a freeze in her chest, gone in a flash. Then, and only then, came the flood of feeling she knew so well.

That tiny jolt has a name, and it turns out to be the most important thing in this entire book. It is the moment DBR is built around. This chapter is about that split second, why it matters so much, and why reaching it can change a reaction that talking never could.

By the end of this chapter, you will understand the single idea that makes Deep Brain Reorienting different from almost everything else. You will learn the difference between the shock that fires first and the emotion that comes second, and why that order matters for healing. You will see why working on the feeling alone can leave a person stuck, and why going back to the earlier moment can loosen something that would not budge before. This is the conceptual heart of the book. Once this clicks, the rest of DBR makes sense.

2.1 The Split Second You Never Notice

Think about the last time something startled you. A door slammed, a car horn blared, someone appeared in a doorway you thought was empty. Before you felt scared, before you even knew what had happened, your body already moved. A flinch. A freeze. A snap of your head toward the sound.

That instant reaction is older than emotion. It runs on ancient machinery deep in the brain, and it is fast because it evolved to keep animals alive in a world full of things that eat them. There is no time to feel afraid before you react. The reaction comes first. The feeling catches up.

Frank Corrigan's core insight was that trauma might get its grip in exactly that instant, the one we never notice because it is over before awareness arrives. He called the deep, pre emotional part of the response by a careful name, and proposed that the sequence of what happens in those first moments is where some trauma gets stored (Corrigan & Christie-Sands, 2020). Not in the story. Not even in the fear. In the flinch before the fear.

Layla had spent years working on the fear and the story. Both real, both worth addressing. But the flinch behind her eyes had never been touched, because she never knew it was there. It fired every time, unhealed, and dragged the whole familiar reaction along behind it.

2.2 Shock Is Not the Same as Fear

Here is a distinction worth slowing down for, because everyday language blurs it. We use the word *shock* loosely, as in that was a shock. DBR uses it in a sharper way.

Shock, in this approach, is the body's instant registration that something unexpected and possibly threatening just happened. It is physical and it is fast. It hits before any emotion has formed. Corrigan describes it as arriving before affect, using the word **affect** as the clinical term for feeling or emotion (Corrigan & Christie-Sands, 2020). So the sequence goes shock first, then affect. First the flinch, then the fear.

Why does this matter? Because most therapy, sensibly, works on affect. It helps people feel their feelings, understand them, and move through them. That is good work. But if the shock underneath never gets processed, the feeling keeps getting re triggered from below, like a fire that keeps reigniting because nobody found the ember.

Put another way, imagine trying to calm a car alarm by arguing with the noise. The noise is real and loud, but it is a symptom. The trigger is a sensor somewhere you have not checked. DBR goes looking for the sensor. It treats the shock as the thing that keeps setting off the alarm, and it works there rather than only with the sound.

You might think this is the same as any body based therapy, since a lot of approaches talk about the nervous system now. It overlaps, but the specific claim is narrower and stranger. DBR is not just saying the body matters. It is saying there is a precise early moment, the shock before the feeling, and that returning to it in the right order is what allows deep healing.

2.3 Example

Meet Diego. He is a college student who freezes during exams. Not ordinary nerves. A full shutdown, mind blank, hands cold, the page swimming. He had tried everything reasonable. Study strategies, breathing apps, a tutor, a talk with a counselor about test anxiety.

The moment it always showed up was the same. He would sit down, flip the exam over, and read the first question. Somewhere in that flip and first glance, the shutdown began. By the time he noticed it, he was already gone, and the rest was damage control.

What he had tried was working on the anxiety, which everyone had called the problem. Breathe through the anxiety. Reframe the anxious thoughts. Reassure the anxious part. None of it reached the freeze, because the freeze was not anxiety. It was something faster and older that happened before the anxiety, in the instant the page turned.

Working with a DBR trained therapist, Diego went back to the flip of the page and found it, a jolt of shock and a hard freeze that landed a half second before any thought. Staying gently with that early moment, over a few sessions, the freeze began to soften. The anxiety was still there sometimes, but the trapdoor under it had closed.

What this means for you: The thing everyone calls the problem is sometimes the second thing, not the first. The first thing is usually a fast physical moment nobody thought to look for.

2.4 Why the Order Matters

There is a reason DBR is so insistent about sequence, about going shock first and affect second, in the order they originally happened.

The nervous system laid the trauma down in an order. Something happened, the deep brain reacted in a split second, and then feeling and meaning piled on top. If you try to heal from the top down, working on the meaning and then the feeling, you are working backward up the stack, and you may never reach the bottom layer that started it all. DBR tries to go in the same order the brain did, reaching the early shock and letting the sequence complete the way it could not at the time (Corrigan & Christie-Sands, 2020).

Think of it like untangling a knot. If you yank on the loose end you can see, the knot often tightens. To actually loosen it, you have to find where the tangle started and work from there. The visible feelings are the loose end. The shock is where the tangle started.

This is also why DBR can feel gentle even though it deals with heavy material. When you reach the early shock directly, you often do not have to relive the whole flooding emotion to get relief. Corrigan and his colleagues argue that working at this deep level can reduce the risk of a person getting overwhelmed, because you are anchoring below the flood rather than swimming through it (Kearney et al., 2023). We will look hard at that claim later. For now, notice the logic. Right layer, right order, less thrashing.

2.5 Example

Meet Aisha. She is a new mother who loves her baby fiercely and yet feels a spike of panic every time the baby cries in a certain pitch. The panic embarrasses her. Good mothers, she tells herself, do not flinch from their own child.

The moment was specific. A particular high, sudden cry, and her whole system would lurch before she could soothe either the baby or herself. She had assumed it was exhaustion, or hormones, or some failing in her.

What she tried was reasoning with herself. The baby is fine. This is normal. Calm down. The reasoning never landed, because the lurch was not a thought she could argue with. It was a shock response firing below the level of thought, and words could not reach it.

In therapy she discovered that the sudden cry echoed something much older, a sound from her own childhood home. The DBR work did not require her to excavate the whole childhood story. It let her return to the instant of shock the cry set off, and stay with it until it settled. The next time the baby wailed, the lurch was smaller. Then smaller still.

What this means for you: A reaction that seems irrational usually is not. It is a fast, old response doing exactly what it learned to do. You cannot argue it away, but it can be reached and settled.

2.6 What This Means for Healing

Step back and take in the shape of the idea. If some trauma lives in the shock before the feeling, then reaching that shock is not a nice extra. It is the missing piece for a certain kind of stuckness.

That is a genuinely hopeful thought, and it explains the quiet excitement around DBR among therapists who work with the hardest cases. It offers a reason why some people never fully healed. They were doing real work, but on the wrong layer, or in the wrong order. Not their fault. Not their therapist's fault. Just a layer the field had not learned to reach yet.

Hold the hope loosely though. Reaching the shock is delicate work, and it is why DBR is done with a trained professional rather than a book or an app. The same depth that makes it powerful makes it something to approach with care and support. You are not meant to go find your own earliest shock alone tonight. If this chapter made you curious about your own reactions, that curiosity is a great reason to seek a skilled therapist, not a reason to start digging by yourself.

The idea is simple to say and hard to do. Shock before feeling. First layer, first. That sentence is the seed of everything else in this book.

2.7 When It Doesn't Work

The most common trap with this idea is deciding that every reaction you have is a hidden shock waiting to be uncovered. It is a seductive lens, and it is not always true.

Here is why it goes wrong. Not all distress is old trauma firing from the deep brain. Sometimes you are anxious because your life is genuinely stressful right now. Sometimes sadness is just grief doing its honest work. Treating every ordinary feeling as a buried shock can send you hunting for a deep cause that is not there, and miss the real, present day thing that needs care.

Three things to try if you find yourself over applying the idea:

1. Ask if the reaction fits the present situation. If your stress matches a genuinely stressful week, it may not need deep excavation. It may need rest, help, or a change you already know about.
2. Look for the tell of a locked shock, which is a reaction that is much bigger or faster than the situation warrants and that does not respond to reason. That mismatch is the signal, not the mere presence of a feeling.
3. Bring the question to a professional rather than diagnosing yourself. Sorting present day feeling from old shock is exactly the kind of thing a trained clinician helps with.

If the whole distinction feels slippery right now, let it be slippery. It gets clearer as we go. You do not have to master it in one chapter.

2.8 What to Take Away

The one idea to carry out of this chapter is the order. Shock first, feeling second. In a moment of threat, the deep brain reacts in a split second, before any emotion forms. DBR calls that instant registration shock, and it uses the word affect for the feeling that follows.

Most therapy works on affect, on the feeling and the story, which is good and helpful work. But if the shock underneath never gets processed, it keeps re triggering the feeling from below, like an ember that keeps restarting a fire. DBR goes looking for the ember.

It reaches the early shock and lets the original sequence complete in the order it first happened.

That is why order matters. The trauma was laid down bottom to top, so healing may need to reach the bottom layer rather than working only on the top. Done well, this can feel gentler than reliving the whole flood, because you are anchoring beneath it.

Two cautions balance the hope. Not every feeling is a hidden shock, so do not turn the idea into a hammer that sees nails everywhere. And reaching real shock is delicate work meant for a trained therapist, not a solo project. Hold the idea, stay curious, and let the next chapters build it out.

Chapter 3.0: Inside The Deep Brain

Hassan was hiking a trail he had walked a hundred times when his body threw him backward before he knew why. His heart was already pounding. His arm was already up. And there on the path, right where his next step would have landed, was a curled shape that his eyes were still catching up to. A stick. Just a bent stick that happened to look like a snake.

Here is the strange part. Hassan jumped first and figured out it was a stick second. His body had decided there was a snake and acted on it a full moment before the thinking part of his brain got a good look and said, relax, it is wood.

That gap, that tiny lag between the body reacting and the mind understanding, is not a flaw. It is one of the oldest and smartest features you own. There is a part of your brain that reacts to possible danger faster than you can think, because thinking is slow and snakes are quick. It would rather make you jump at ten sticks than let you step on one snake.

That fast, ancient part is where Deep Brain Reorienting does its work. In this chapter we are going to take a short, friendly tour of it. You will not have to memorize anything. You will just meet a few key players, get a feel for what each one does, and see why they matter for healing trauma. By the end, words that sound intimidating right now will feel like old acquaintances.

By the end of this chapter you will have a simple, working picture of the deep part of the brain that DBR focuses on. You will meet three main players and know, in plain terms, what each one does in a moment of threat. You will understand why this old machinery reacts before you can think, and why that speed is exactly what makes it matter for trauma. You will not become a neuroscientist, and you do not need to. You will just have a map good enough to follow the rest of the book with confidence.

3.1 The Brain Beneath Thought

You have, in a rough sense, layers of brain that arrived at different points in evolution. The newest, outer layers handle the things you think of as you. Language, planning, reasoning, weighing your options. This is the part that reads a book and makes a shopping list.

Underneath sits much older equipment, near the top of the spinal cord, in a region called the **brainstem** and the areas just above it. This is the part your body shares with creatures that existed long before anything wrote a shopping list. It handles the basics that keep you alive without your input. Breathing. Heart rate. And crucially, the instant reaction to threat.

The important thing to hold is speed. The old brain is fast and the thinking brain is slow. When Hassan jumped at the stick, the old brain ran the show, and the thinking brain arrived late with an explanation. That is normal and healthy. But it also means that when something overwhelming happens, the old brain reacts and stores something before the thinking brain can process it in words. That is a big clue about why some trauma cannot be reached with words alone.

Corrigan built DBR on the idea that this deep region is where certain trauma responses begin, and that healing needs to reach them there (Corrigan & Christie-Sands, 2020). So this is the neighborhood we are visiting. Let's meet the residents.

3.2 The Part That Points

Start with attention. When that stick caught Hassan's eye, something snapped his gaze and his whole head toward it. That snapping toward is called the **orienting response**, and a small structure deep in the brain helps drive it. In the science it is called the **superior colliculi**, which is a mouthful, so just think of it as the pointing part.

Its job is to answer one urgent question. Where? Where is the movement, the sound, the possible threat? It swivels your attention toward it before you have decided anything. You have felt this a thousand times. A movement at the edge of your vision, and your eyes go there on their own. Someone says your name across a noisy room, and your head turns before you choose to turn it.

This pointing part matters enormously for trauma, because in a shocking moment, the very first thing that happens is this orienting. The body turns toward the threat. Corrigan proposes that this early orienting, and the tension that comes with it, is part of what gets locked in when an experience is too much (Corrigan & Christie-Sands, 2020). We will spend all of the next chapter on that tension, because it is the doorway DBR uses. For now, just meet the pointing part and remember its one word question. Where.

3.3 Example

Meet Nicole. She is a schoolteacher who noticed that she could not watch certain scenes on television, the ones with a sudden reveal of someone standing in a doorway. Her body would jolt hard, out of proportion to a show she knew was fake.

The moment was always the same. The character turns, and someone is there who should not be. In that instant Nicole's head would snap and her breath would catch, exactly as if the danger were in her own living room.

What she had tried was avoidance. She simply stopped watching anything with suspense, which shrank her world a little more each year. She also tried telling herself it was only a show, which never helped, because the jolt was faster than any sentence she could say.

In therapy she learned that her pointing part was doing its job too well, snapping her toward a threat that echoed something real from her past. The reaction was not weakness. It was an old orienting response firing on a modern trigger. Naming it that way did not fix it, but it stopped her from feeling broken, and it gave her therapist a precise place to work.

What this means for you: A jolt toward a harmless trigger is not you being fragile. It is the pointing part of your brain doing an ancient job on a false alarm.

3.4 The Alarm Chemical

Once your attention has snapped toward a possible threat, your body needs to get ready fast. That is the second player. Deep in the brainstem is a small spot that, when it fires, floods your system with a chemical that acts like an alarm bell. The spot is called the **locus coeruleus**, and the chemical is **noradrenaline**, which you can think of as the body's alert signal.

When the alarm chemical releases, your heart speeds, your muscles ready, your whole body shifts into high alert. This happens in a flash, and here is the part that connects straight back to Chapter 2. It happens before you feel afraid. Corrigan describes this burst as part of the **shock** response, the rapid physical alert that arrives before any emotion has formed (Corrigan & Christie-Sands, 2020). First the alarm chemical, then, a beat later, the feeling of fear.

This is why the shock before feeling is not just a poetic idea. It maps onto real machinery. There is an actual alarm system that fires faster than emotion, and DBR is built to work with what it leaves behind. When that alarm fires during an overwhelming event and never fully settles, it can leave a kind of residue, a body that stays a little too ready, a little too alert, for years.

You do not need to remember the name locus coeruleus. You just need the idea. There is an alarm that goes off before the fear, and its leftover charge is part of what keeps a person stuck.

3.5 The Part That Braces

The third player handles what happens when threat is close and the body has to do something about it. Just above the brainstem sits a region called the **periaqueductal gray**, which we can simply call the bracing part.

This is the part involved in the deep, automatic survival responses. The freeze that locks you in place. The urge to fight or flee. The bracing for impact. Researchers have found that this region is organized to produce different survival reactions depending on the situation, and it is closely tied to how strong emotions get expressed in the body (Corrigan & Christie-Sands, 2020). Where the pointing part asks where and the alarm chemical says get ready, the bracing part decides, in effect, what do we do to survive this.

For trauma, this matters because so many trauma responses are survival responses that got stuck partway through. A freeze that never got to unfreeze. A run that never got to finish. Peter Levine, who developed a body based trauma approach, described trauma partly as survival energy that got locked in the body because the response could not complete (Levine, 1997). DBR shares that instinct and adds a precise focus on reaching the early part of the sequence, in the deep brain, where it all began.

So there is your cast. The pointing part that turns you toward threat. The alarm chemical that gets you ready. The bracing part that runs survival. Three players, one fast sequence, all older than thought.

3.6 Example

Meet Ravi. He survived a serious car accident and, on the surface, recovered well. No broken bones that lasted, no obvious flashbacks. But he could not sit in the passenger seat of a car without a full body clench, a bracing so strong that his legs ached afterward.

The moment was every time someone else drove and had to brake even gently. His body would slam into a brace, feet pressing an invisible pedal, whole frame rigid, long before he consciously registered the car slowing.

What he had tried was willpower. He told himself he was safe, that this driver was careful, that the accident was over. The bracing ignored him completely, because it was not coming from the part of the brain that listens to reason. It was coming from the bracing part, still finishing a survival response that got frozen at the moment of impact.

Understanding this changed how Ravi's therapist worked with him. Instead of arguing with the brace, the DBR trained clinician helped him return to the early moment in the deep brain sequence and let the frozen response slowly complete. The clench did not vanish overnight, but over sessions his body began to trust that the impact was truly over.

What this means for you: A body that braces or freezes is not being dramatic. It is a survival response that got stuck partway through and never got the signal that the danger passed.

3.7 Why The Map Matters

You might be wondering why any of this brain tour matters if you are never going to use the names. Here is why. DBR is not a vague promise to work with the body. It is a specific claim that certain trauma lives in this deep, fast machinery, and that you can reach it by following the same sequence the brain used. The map is the reason the method exists.

There is an honest catch, and the people who created DBR say it plainly. A lot of this deep brain picture is still hypothesis. We cannot open a living brain mid trauma and watch these parts light up in order. Corrigan and his colleagues are upfront that the model is a set of well reasoned ideas that appear to be clinically useful, not a fully proven diagram (Corrigan & Christie-Sands, 2020). Some readers of the main academic book have specifically praised the authors for being honest that the brainstem details are hypothetical while still helpful in practice.

That honesty is a good sign, not a bad one. A method that says here is our best current map, and here is what we are still unsure about, is being straight with you. Hold the map as a useful guide rather than gospel. It is good enough to work from, which is all a map has to be.

3.8 When It Doesn't Work

The most common way this chapter trips people up is the feeling that you have to master the brain science to benefit, and that if the names slide out of your head, you have failed. You have not.

Here is why the worry is misplaced. You do not drive a car by naming its engine parts, and you do not heal trauma by memorizing brain regions. The names are scaffolding. They help you follow the logic. Once the logic lands, you can let the names go, the same way you forget the plot of a movie but keep how it made you feel.

Three things to try if the science feels slippery:

1. Skip the names and keep the jobs. Pointing part, alarm chemical, bracing part. That plain version carries everything you actually need.
2. Reread only the two real examples in this chapter. The stories hold the concepts better than the definitions do.

3. Trust that it compounds. Each later chapter reuses these ideas, so they sink in through repetition without any effort from you.

If the whole tour felt like too much, close the book for today. None of this is going anywhere, and it reads easier the second time.

3.9 What to Remember

Underneath your thinking brain sits much older equipment in and just above the brainstem. It reacts to threat faster than you can think, which is why Hassan jumped at the stick before he knew it was wood. That speed is a feature, and it is also why some trauma gets stored before words can reach it.

Three players run the fast reaction. The pointing part, the superior colliculi, snaps your attention toward a threat and asks where. The alarm chemical, noradrenaline released by the locus coeruleus, floods your body to get ready, and it fires before fear, which is the shock before feeling made physical. The bracing part, the periaqueductal gray, runs the deep survival responses, the freeze and the brace that so often get stuck partway through.

DBR is built on the claim that certain trauma lives in this deep, fast sequence, and that healing can reach it there. The people who created DBR are honest that much of this map is still hypothesis, well reasoned and clinically useful rather than fully proven. That honesty is a strength.

You do not need the names. Keep the jobs and the stories. Pointing part, alarm chemical, bracing part, all older than thought. That is plenty to carry forward.

Chapter 4.0: The Orienting Moment

Sofia was sitting across from her therapist, trying to describe why a certain coworker unsettled her, when the therapist asked her to pause and notice her own body. Not her thoughts about the coworker. Her body, right then.

Sofia went quiet. And slowly she became aware of something she had never once noticed in her whole life. A faint pull of tension across her forehead and around her eyes, and a slight stiffening at the back of her neck, as if some part of her were straining to look at something. It had been there the whole time she was talking. It was probably there a lot of the time. She had simply never turned her attention to it.

That small, almost invisible tension is the center of everything in Deep Brain Reorienting. It is the thread the whole method pulls on. Most people carry it and never notice it, the same way you do not notice your tongue resting in your mouth until someone mentions it. But once you learn to feel it, it becomes a doorway to the earliest layer of a reaction.

This chapter is about that tension. Where it comes from, what it means, and why staying with it, instead of the story attached to it, is the surprising move at the heart of DBR. This is the most hands on chapter so far, in the sense that you will start to feel what the work actually involves.

By the end of this chapter you will understand what orienting tension is and where to feel it in the body. You will learn what sets it off, and why DBR asks people to stay with the raw physical tension rather than the thoughts and feelings on top of it. You will see how this quiet tension can become a stable anchor, a way to stay grounded in the present while touching something old. You will finish with a clear feel for the raw material DBR works with, which sets up the next chapter, where we walk through an actual session step by step.

4.1 The Hidden Tension

Go back to Chapter 3 for a second. When the pointing part of your brain snaps your attention toward something, that turn is not only in your eyes. It runs through the small muscles of your face, your head, and your neck. A readiness. A subtle bracing to look, to track, to see what is there.

Corrigan gave this a name. **Orienting tension**. It is the physical signature of your deep brain turning toward something that matters, and it shows up most clearly in the face, the head, and the neck (Corrigan & Christie-Sands, 2020). Usually it is so faint and so fast that it never reaches your awareness. It flickers and fades under the louder waves of feeling that follow.

But it is there. And in a moment of shock, that orienting tension can get caught, held in the body as part of the locked sequence. Long after the event, when something reminds the deep brain of the old threat, the same tension can quietly reappear, a small strain in the face or neck, underneath whatever emotion you consciously feel.

The reason this matters so much is timing. The tension belongs to the earliest part of the reaction, the orienting, which comes before the fear and before the story. If you can find that tension, you have found a thread that leads back to the very beginning of the sequence. That is why DBR treats it as gold.

4.2 What Sets It Off

In a session, a person does not just wait around hoping tension appears. The therapist gives it something to respond to. That something is called the **activating stimulus**, which simply means the trigger you deliberately bring to mind so the deep brain reacts and the tension shows up.

The activating stimulus can be a small piece of a difficult memory, or it can be a present day trigger. It does not have to be the whole overwhelming story. In fact, DBR often works with just a sliver, a single image or a single moment, precisely so the person is not flooded (Corrigan & Christie-Sands, 2020). You bring the sliver to mind, gently, and you watch what the body does.

Think of it like this. If you want to find a small leak, you turn the water on just a little and watch for the drip. You do not blast the pipe at full pressure. The activating stimulus is that careful trickle. It is enough to make the orienting tension appear so you can work with it, without turning on the full flood of the memory.

This careful dosing is a big part of why DBR can feel gentler than methods that ask a person to relive an event in full. You are not reliving. You are bringing just enough of the trigger to make the earliest physical response show itself, then turning your attention to that response.

4.3 Example

Meet Miguel. He came to therapy because of a persistent sense of dread around authority figures, especially older men in positions of power. He could not trace it to any single dramatic event, which frustrated him.

The moment his therapist chose as an activating stimulus was small and specific. Miguel pictured the face of a former boss, just the face, just for a second. He was not asked to relive any particular argument or scene, only to hold that one image lightly.

What he tried at first was what most people try, which is to launch into the story. He started explaining what the boss had done, why it was unfair, how it made him feel. His therapist gently redirected him, again and again, away from the narrative and toward his body.

What worked was when Miguel finally noticed a tightening high in his chest and a pull at the front of his throat as he held the image. He stayed with just that, the tightening and the pull, saying almost nothing. Within a few minutes the sensation shifted and eased, and a wave of old, quiet grief moved through and passed.

What this means for you: The story feels like the important part, and it is not where this work happens. The body's small, early signal is the thread that actually moves things.

4.4 Staying With The Tension

Here is the part that surprises almost everyone, so let's slow down on it. In DBR, when the orienting tension appears, the instruction is essentially to stay with it. Not to analyze it. Not to talk about the memory. Not to push it away or breathe it out. Just to keep your attention on the raw physical tension and let it do what it needs to do.

This runs against every instinct. When we feel discomfort, we want to explain it, fix it, or escape it. DBR asks for something quieter. You turn toward the sensation with curiosity and you keep it company. The idea is that the deep brain, given gentle attention and time, can move through the sequence it got stuck in and settle it (Corrigan & Christie-Sands, 2020).

Why does staying with the sensation, rather than the story, work better here? Because the story lives in the thinking brain, and we already know the thinking brain is not where this trauma is stuck. The tension lives in the deep brain, in the exact spot that needs to complete its sequence. Keep your attention on the story and you are talking to the wrong floor of the building. Keep it on the tension and you are finally in the right room.

This is also the reason DBR is done with a trained guide. Staying with raw physical tension from an old shock can bring up a lot. A skilled therapist knows how to keep the dose small, how to pace it, and how to help if the person starts to get overwhelmed. It looks simple from the outside. It is not simple to do well.

4.5 Example

Meet Amara. She had a lifelong habit of freezing in conflict. The instant anyone raised their voice, she went blank and could not speak, then felt ashamed about it for days.

Her therapist used a gentle activating stimulus, asking Amara to recall just the sound of a raised voice, not any full argument. Amara immediately felt a hard stillness come over the muscles of her jaw and the back of her skull, a locking, as if her whole head had braced.

What she had done for years was fight the freeze. She read articles on being assertive, rehearsed comebacks, and criticized herself for going quiet. None of it reached the freeze, because the freeze was a deep brain response, not a lack of good scripts.

What worked was staying with the locking sensation itself, without trying to unlock it by force. She kept her attention on the braced stillness in her jaw and skull, and let it be there. Slowly, over more than one session, the lock began to loosen on its own, and she found small moments where words came in situations that used to silence her.

What this means for you: You cannot script your way out of a deep freeze. But the frozen tension itself, given patient attention with the right support, can begin to thaw.

4.6 An Anchor In The Present

There is one more thing the orienting tension does, and it is beautiful in its simplicity. It keeps a person anchored in the present while they touch something from the past.

A big risk in any trauma work is that a person gets swept away, pulled so far into an old memory that they lose contact with the safe room they are actually sitting in. DBR guards against this in a clever way. Because the orienting tension is a real, physical sensation happening right now, in this body, in this moment, focusing on it keeps one foot firmly in the present. Corrigan describes this deep attention to the tension as a way of staying grounded, so the person is neither swept away by high intensity emotion nor split off into a frozen part cut off from the present (Corrigan & Christie-Sands, 2020).

Put another way, the tension is both the doorway and the handrail. It leads back to the early moment of the reaction, and at the same time it gives the person something solid and present to hold onto so they do not fall in. That double role is a lot of why the method can reach deep material without flooding people.

You are not meant to try this alone tonight, and I will keep saying that, kindly, because it is true. But you can begin to notice your own orienting tension in ordinary life, the small pull in your face or neck when something catches your attention. Noticing it is harmless and interesting. Working with an old, painful version of it is the part that calls for a trained companion.

4.7 When It Doesn't Work

The most common snag is that a person tries to find their orienting tension and feels absolutely nothing. Blank. No pull, no tightness, no sensation at all. This is incredibly common and it is not a failure.

Here is why it happens. Many people, especially those who survived a lot, learned long ago to tune out body sensations because the body was not a safe place to feel. That tuning out was protective. It kept them functioning. So of course the signal is faint at first. The skill of noticing it comes back slowly, with patience and usually with help.

Three things to try if you feel nothing:

1. Lower the stakes. Instead of hunting for tension around a hard memory, just practice noticing any body sensation at all, warmth in your hands, weight in your feet. The noticing muscle strengthens with easy reps first.
2. Give it time in a session, not alone. A trained therapist has gentle ways to help the signal surface safely that are hard to do by yourself.
3. Do not force it. Straining to feel makes the signal hide. A soft, patient curiosity works far better than effort.

If your body still feels like a locked room, that is worth real gentleness and probably professional support. A closed off body is not a broken one. It is a protected one, and protection can ease when it feels safe to.

4.8 The Short Answer

Orienting tension is the small physical signature of your deep brain turning toward something that matters, felt mostly in the face, head, and neck. It usually flickers past unnoticed, but in a shocking moment it can get caught and held, quietly reappearing whenever the old threat is echoed.

In a session, a therapist offers an activating stimulus, a small piece of a memory or a present trigger, just enough to make that tension show up without flooding the person. Then comes the move that surprises everyone. You stay with the raw tension itself, not the story, because the tension lives in the deep brain where the trauma is stuck, and the story lives in the thinking brain where it is not.

The tension serves double duty. It is the doorway back to the earliest moment of the reaction, and it is the handrail that keeps a person anchored in the present so they are not swept away. That is much of why DBR can reach deep material gently.

If you try to find your tension and feel nothing, that is common and not a failure. A body that learned to tune out sensation for protection needs patience, easy practice, and usually a trained guide before the signal returns.

Chapter 5.0: Inside A DBR Session

Yuki almost canceled her first session three times. She had read a little about Deep Brain Reorienting and could not picture what she was walking into. Would she have to relive the worst day of her life out loud? Would she cry in front of a stranger? Would there be some intense technique, lights or tapping or a script she had to follow?

What she found was quieter than any of that. A calm room. A therapist who explained everything first and asked permission at each step. No pressure to tell the whole story. Long stretches of simply sitting with her eyes closed, noticing her own body, while the therapist waited beside her with unhurried patience. At one point Yuki opened her eyes and said, is this it? Am I doing it right? And her therapist smiled and said yes, this quiet is exactly it.

Most people carry a dramatic picture of trauma therapy, all catharsis and breakthrough. A real DBR session tends to look almost boring from the outside, which is part of why it can be so kind to the nervous system. In this chapter we are going to sit in on a session together, step by step, so the mystery goes away and you know what actually happens in that room.

By the end of this chapter you will be able to picture a Deep Brain Reorienting session from beginning to end. You will know what the room feels like, how the therapist finds a starting point, what the person does through the middle of the work, and what usually happens by the end. You will meet the simple sequence that runs underneath it all. You will also get a realistic sense of how many sessions this tends to take and what results look like, so your expectations match reality rather than a movie version of healing.

5.1 What The Room Feels Like

The first thing to know is that a DBR session is slow and collaborative. It is not something done to you. The therapist explains the approach, answers your questions, and checks that you actually want to proceed before anything begins. You stay in charge the whole way.

The pace is unhurried on purpose. There are long, quiet pauses. The therapist is comfortable with silence, because the silence is where the work happens. You are not being tested and there is no performance. Much of the time your eyes may be closed while you turn your attention inward, and the therapist sits with you, occasionally offering a gentle question or a steadying word.

Sessions are often done in person, but they also work well over video. In the main research study, people received Deep Brain Reorienting entirely through videoconferencing, and it still helped (Kearney et al., 2023). So the room might literally be your own living room, with the therapist on a screen. What matters is not the setting but the quiet, careful quality of attention.

If you were expecting intensity, this calm can feel almost anticlimactic at first, the way Yuki wondered if she was doing it right. That calm is not a sign that nothing is happening. It is the whole design. The gentleness is what lets the deep brain feel safe enough to move.

5.2 Finding The Starting Point

Every session needs a place to begin, and the therapist helps find it. This is where the activating stimulus from the last chapter comes in. Together, you and the therapist choose a small, specific trigger to work with. It might be a sliver of a memory, a single image, or a present day situation that reliably stirs something up.

The key word is small. The therapist is not looking to crack open your whole history at once. They want just enough of a trigger to make your deep brain respond, so the orienting tension appears and there is something real to work with. Choosing a manageable starting point is a skill, and it is one of the ways a trained clinician keeps the work safe (Corrigan & Christie-Sands, 2020).

Once you have a starting point, the therapist invites you to bring it lightly to mind and then, almost immediately, to notice your body. Where is the tension? What is happening in your face, your head, your neck, your chest? The focus moves off the trigger and onto the physical response the trigger produced. The trigger was just the match. The tension is the flame you actually tend.

From here, the talking mostly stops, and the quieter middle of the session begins.

5.3 Example

Meet David. He is a firefighter who came to DBR for recurring nightmares tied to a warehouse fire where a colleague was badly hurt. He was skeptical of anything that sounded soft, and he agreed to try mostly because nothing else had helped the sleep.

For the starting point, his therapist did not ask him to recount the fire. She asked him to bring to mind just the split second when he first heard the sound of the ceiling giving way, and to hold only that, briefly. Then she asked him to notice his body.

What David tried to do, out of habit, was narrate. He started giving the operational rundown, positions and timing and what went wrong, the way he would in a debrief. His therapist gently guided him back each time, toward the sensation, away from the report.

What worked was when he finally caught it, a violent tension gripping his shoulders and the base of his neck, the physical shape of bracing for that sound. He stayed with it, quiet, for several minutes. It rose, shifted, and slowly released, and afterward he described feeling strangely lighter, like setting down a pack he had forgotten he was carrying. His nightmares eased over the following weeks.

What this means for you: Even people trained to handle crisis carry frozen tension from it. Reaching that tension, not retelling the event, is what brings relief.

5.4 The Sequence Underneath

Everything you have learned so far fits into one simple chain, and DBR practitioners sometimes refer to it by the shorthand **O-T-A-S**. You do not need the letters, but the sequence is worth seeing laid out, because it is the spine of the whole method.

First comes orienting. The deep brain turns toward the significant trigger. Then comes the tension, the orienting tension in the face, head, and neck that we spent all of Chapter 4 on. Then comes affect, the emotion that arrives after the tension, the fear or grief or anger. And then comes seeking, the deep pull to reach out for connection that lives in the same old machinery, which is why the shorthand spells out orienting, tension, affect, seeking (Corrigan & Christie-Sands, 2020).

The whole point of DBR is to follow this chain in its natural order, starting at the beginning. Most therapy jumps in at affect, the feeling, which is the third link. DBR backs up to the first links, the orienting and the tension, and works from there. By starting where the sequence started, it lets the deep brain complete the process it could not finish during the original event.

That is really all the middle of a session is. The therapist helps you find the early links, the orienting and the tension, and then keeps you gentle company while your deep brain does the rest at its own pace. It is less like performing a technique and more like giving a stuck sequence the time and safety to finish.

5.5 What Usually Happens

So what does a person actually do during those quiet middle minutes? Mostly, they stay still and pay attention to the tension. Corrigan notes that people often remain quite still while processing these sensations, though sometimes the head moves a little on its own, as if completing the orienting turn it never got to finish (Corrigan & Christie-Sands, 2020). Either way is fine. The body knows what it needs.

As the person stays with the tension, it tends to change. It may build, then shift, then ease. Often an emotion moves through as the affect link of the sequence surfaces and passes. And frequently there is a sense of relief on the other side, a settling, a lightness, sometimes tears that feel like release rather than distress. In the research, people who received Deep Brain Reorienting showed meaningful reductions in trauma symptoms, with the benefits holding up months later (Kearney et al., 2023).

How many sessions does this take? There is no fixed number, and it depends on the person and the complexity of what they bring. As a rough anchor, the main study worked with eight sessions and saw significant results (Kearney et al., 2023). Some people notice shifts sooner. Complex, layered trauma generally takes longer and unfolds across more sessions. Anyone promising a one and done miracle is overselling.

The honest picture is a series of quiet, patient sessions, each one settling a little more of the old sequence, with relief that tends to build and last rather than arriving in a single dramatic burst.

5.6 Example

Meet Jennifer. She sought help for panic attacks that struck without warning, often in ordinary places like grocery stores. She had begun to organize her life around avoiding them, and her world was shrinking.

Her therapist chose a gentle starting point, not a full panic attack but just the first flicker of that too familiar feeling of something is wrong. Jennifer brought that flicker to mind and turned her attention to her body.

What she had done for years was fight panic with logic and distraction, counting backward, gripping her keys, telling herself there was no real danger. It sometimes got her through a moment, but it never reduced how often panic came, because it never touched the deep sequence underneath.

What worked in DBR was staying with the very first bodily sign, a subtle tension around her eyes and a flutter high in her stomach, before the panic could build. Over several sessions, meeting the sequence at its start rather than fighting it at its peak, the attacks grew less frequent and less fierce, and her world slowly widened again.

What this means for you: Meeting a reaction at its quiet beginning is often far more effective than battling it once it has grown loud.

5.7 When It Doesn't Work

The most common early snag is a session where, from your point of view, nothing seems to happen. You sat, you noticed some tension, and there was no big wave, no tears, no obvious shift. It is easy to conclude it is not working.

Here is why that judgment is usually wrong. DBR is quiet by nature, and real change in the deep brain is not always dramatic or immediately obvious. Some of the most useful sessions feel understated in the moment, and the effects show up later as a trigger that has quietly lost some of its charge. Corrigan and colleagues are also honest that the practice can be difficult and that it does not work for everyone, so a slow start is not a verdict (Corrigan & Christie-Sands, 2020).

Three things to try if a session feels flat:

1. Give it a few sessions before you judge. The skill of finding and staying with tension grows, and so does the payoff.
2. Notice small changes in daily life rather than big moments in the room. Slightly better sleep, a trigger that stings a little less. That is the work landing.
3. Tell your therapist honestly that it feels flat. Pacing and starting points can be adjusted, and that feedback helps.

And if, after a fair try with a skilled clinician, DBR simply is not the right fit for you, that is real information, not failure. It does not work for everyone, and there are other good approaches. A later chapter looks at how DBR compares to them.

5.8 Pulling It Together

A Deep Brain Reorienting session is slower and quieter than most people expect. It is collaborative, permission based, and often full of long, comfortable silences. It can happen in person or over video, since the research showed it working well even entirely online.

The therapist helps you find a small starting point, an activating stimulus, then guides your attention off the trigger and onto the orienting tension in your body. Underneath it all runs a simple sequence, sometimes shortened to O-T-A-S. Orienting, then tension, then affect, then seeking, tracked in order. Most therapy starts at the feeling. DBR backs up to the beginning and lets the deep brain complete the sequence it once got stuck in.

Through the quiet middle of a session, a person mostly stays still and keeps attention on the tension, which tends to build, shift, and ease, often with an emotion moving through and relief on the far side. There is no fixed number of sessions. The main study used eight and saw lasting benefit, while complex trauma usually takes longer.

If a session feels flat, that is common and not a verdict, since DBR is understated by design and does not suit everyone. Give it a fair try with a skilled guide, watch for small changes in daily life, and keep your therapist honest company in the process.

Chapter 6.0: Where Attachment Shock Lives

Omar had what everyone would call a good childhood. No violence, no disaster, no single terrible day he could point to. His parents provided, showed up to his games, and told him they loved him. And yet, as an adult, he could not let anyone get close without a part of him quietly bracing, as if intimacy itself were a kind of threat.

It confused him and, honestly, embarrassed him. When people talk about trauma, they mean something dramatic, and nothing dramatic had happened to him. So he assumed his trouble with closeness was just his personality, a flaw he was stuck with, evidence that he was cold or broken in some way he could not name.

Here is what Omar did not know. The kind of wound that shaped him does not always come from a big event. Sometimes it comes from small, fast moments in early relationships. A caregiver who turned away at the wrong instant. A look of disappointment that landed before a child had words for it. A sudden coldness where warmth was expected. These moments can register as a kind of shock, deep and early, long before they become any story a person could tell.

Deep Brain Reorienting has a specific name for this, and a specific way of understanding it. This chapter is about that quieter kind of wound, the sort that hides inside people who insist nothing bad ever happened to them. If you have ever felt broken for reasons you cannot explain, this may be the most important chapter in the book.

By the end of this chapter you will understand what attachment shock is and why it can shape a person even without any obvious traumatic event. You will learn the difference between two kinds of early relational hurt, and why the fast, pre emotional kind is so easy to miss. You will see how these early moments can quietly set patterns that run through an entire adult life. You will finish with a kinder and more accurate picture of your own relational struggles, and a sense of why DBR reaches this material when talking about your childhood often does not.

6.1 When Nothing Bad Happened

A lot of people rule themselves out of trauma work because their suffering does not come with a dramatic origin story. My childhood was fine, they say. Others had it so much worse. And so they carry a private ache they never bring to anyone, because it does not seem to qualify.

This is one of the quiet tragedies in how we talk about trauma. We picture the big, obvious wounds and miss the small, early ones that can be just as formative. A child does not need a catastrophe to be shaped by a relationship. They need only the ordinary, repeated experience of reaching for connection and, sometimes, not finding it in the way they needed.

DBR takes these early relational moments seriously. Corrigan's work describes an innate system deep in the brain that drives us to seek closeness with others from the very beginning of life, building on older accounts of the brain's seeking and care systems (Corrigan & Christie-Sands, 2020; Panksepp, 1998). When that reaching for closeness meets a sudden absence, a turning away, a coldness, it can produce a jolt in that deep system. Not a dramatic event. A fast, wordless moment that the deep brain registers and files away.

Omar's childhood really was fine in all the visible ways. But somewhere in it were small moments of reaching and not being met, and his deep brain had kept the record long after his thinking mind forgot the details.

6.2 The Two Kinds Of Hurt

DBR draws a useful distinction between two ways an early relationship can wound. Corrigan describes attachment trauma as coming from two main experiences, which we can call **shock** and **pain** (Corrigan & Christie-Sands, 2020).

Pain is the part we usually recognize. It is the hurt of not being loved well, the sadness and longing and anger that build up over time. Pain has a feeling to it, and we can often talk about it, even if it is hard.

Shock is the sneakier one, and it is the piece DBR is especially built to reach. Attachment shock is that fast, pre emotional jolt in the deep brain at the instant of a sudden relational rupture. A parent's face going cold without warning. A caregiver pulling back at the moment a child expected to be caught. It happens too fast for feeling, exactly like the shock we met in Chapter 2, only here the threat is not a snake or a crash. The threat is the sudden loss of connection.

Because shock comes before feeling and before words, it is almost impossible to reach by talking about your childhood. You can describe the pain for years and never touch the shock underneath, because the shock was never a story in the first place. It was a jolt. DBR goes after the jolt.

This distinction is why some people do years of insightful therapy about their family and still feel the same old bracing around closeness. They were working on the pain, which is real and worth it, while the shock sat untouched below.

6.3 Example

Meet Isabella. She had a pattern that had wrecked three good relationships. The moment a partner got truly close and loving, she felt an urge to push them away that she could not control or explain.

The moment always came right at the peak of closeness. A partner would say something tender, or reach for her at a vulnerable instant, and instead of melting she would feel a sharp internal recoil, a lurch away, before any thought arrived.

What she had tried was years of talk therapy about her parents, her fear of abandonment, her trust issues. She understood her history in great detail. The understanding was genuine, and it changed nothing about the recoil, because the recoil was not an idea. It was a shock response firing at the exact moment of closeness.

In DBR, her therapist helped her return, gently, to that instant of recoil, using a small activating stimulus rather than reliving whole relationships. Isabella found a hard flinch in her chest and throat that landed the second closeness peaked. Staying with that early flinch, over several sessions, the automatic push began to soften, and she could stay in a tender moment without fleeing.

What this means for you: Understanding your history is valuable and often not enough. The fast bodily recoil underneath a pattern is a different thing, and it needs to be reached where it lives.

6.4 The Reach And The Pull

Here is one of the most human and heartbreaking parts of this whole picture. In a moment of attachment shock, a person can feel two opposite urges at the very same time. The urge to reach toward the other person for comfort, and the urge to pull away to protect themselves.

Corrigan describes exactly this, opposing urges that can be present together in the deep brain's response, a simultaneous pull to reach out and to defend or withdraw (Corrigan & Christie-Sands, 2020). Picture a small child whose parent is both their main source of comfort and the source of a sudden hurt. The child's deep brain wants to run to the parent and away from the parent at once. There is no clean resolution to that, so the two urges get locked together.

This is why so many people feel torn in close relationships in a way that seems irrational. They crave closeness and they flee it. They want to be held and they cannot bear to be held. It is not indecision or game playing. It is two ancient urges, reach and pull, wired together in the same instant of old shock.

Once you see this, a lot of confusing relationship behavior in yourself and others starts to make sad, clear sense. The reach and the pull are not a character defect. They are the fingerprint of an early moment when connection and threat arrived together.

6.5 Example

Meet Fatima. She described herself as terrible at receiving care. When she was sick or struggling and someone tried to help her, she felt an almost unbearable discomfort and would insist she was fine, then feel lonely that no one helped.

The moment showed up whenever kindness was aimed directly at her. A friend offering real support, and Fatima's whole system would tighten and deflect, even as another part of her ached to accept it.

What she had done was label herself as fiercely independent and leave it there. The label was a story that covered the discomfort without touching it. Underneath, being cared for actually triggered a small alarm, because early on, moments of needing care had come with a jolt of being let down.

Working in DBR, Fatima met the tightening that arose the instant care was offered, and stayed with it. Slowly the reach and the pull began to loosen their grip on each other, and she found she could let a friend show up for her without the old recoil taking over.

What this means for you: If receiving love feels strangely threatening, you are not broken or cold. An old shock may have wired care and danger together, and that wiring can change.

6.6 How It Shapes A Life

The reason attachment shock matters so much is that it does not stay in childhood. The deep brain lays down these early sequences, and then repeats them for years, across completely different relationships and situations.

Corrigan notes that sequences established at the brainstem level can underlie patterns of relating that repeat over many years in different contexts (Corrigan & Christie-Sands, 2020). The same reach and pull that formed with a caregiver can replay with partners, friends, and bosses, decades later, with people who had nothing to do with the original moment. Over time, these repeating patterns can become so constant that they look like personality, just who someone is. Decades of work in interpersonal neurobiology describe how early relationships shape the developing mind in exactly this lasting way (Siegel, 2012).

That reframing is powerful. What a person calls I am just bad at closeness or I am too independent or I always sabotage good things may not be fixed personality at all. It may be an old brainstem sequence, still running, still reachable. Personality can feel like destiny. An early shock pattern feels more like something that got set and can be reset.

This is the hope inside a hard chapter. If the thing shaping your relationships is a locked early sequence rather than an unchangeable trait, then there is somewhere to work, and DBR is aimed right at it. Not by talking you out of your patterns, but by reaching the deep moment where they began.

6.7 When It Doesn't Work

The most common way this chapter goes wrong is that it turns into blaming your parents for everything. You start seeing attachment shock behind every difficulty and every caregiver as the villain who caused it. That is a trap.

Here is why it misleads you. Attachment shock is often nobody's fault in any simple way. Caregivers are human, moments of rupture happen in even loving homes, and a jolt in a child's deep brain does not require a bad parent. Turning this understanding into a case against your family usually adds fresh pain without touching the old shock, and it can keep you stuck in resentment.

Three things to try if you find yourself sliding into blame:

1. Hold the difference between cause and blame. A moment can shape you without anyone being a monster. Understanding the origin does not require an indictment.
2. Notice that not every relationship struggle is attachment shock. Some difficulties are present day, about the actual people in front of you now, and need present day work.
3. Bring the sorting to a professional. Telling old shock from current conflict from ordinary human friction is exactly what a skilled therapist helps with.

If this chapter stirred up grief about your childhood, that grief is real and deserves care, not a solo excavation. Let it be a reason to seek support, not a reason to reopen everything alone.

6.8 The Main Ideas

Attachment shock is a fast, pre emotional jolt in the deep brain that happens when a reach for connection meets a sudden rupture, a turning away, a coldness, a moment of not being caught. It can shape a person deeply even without any dramatic event, which is why people with fine childhoods sometimes carry real relational wounds.

DBR distinguishes two kinds of early hurt. Pain, which has feeling and can often be talked about, and shock, which comes before feeling and words and is nearly impossible to reach by discussing your history. Talking works on the pain. DBR goes after the shock.

In a moment of attachment shock, a person can feel two opposite urges at once, to reach toward the other and to pull away, wired together. This reach and pull explains a lot of confusing relationship behavior that looks irrational but is really an old sequence firing.

These early sequences repeat for years and can harden into what looks like personality. The hope is that a pattern set by shock can be reset by reaching it, rather than being a fixed trait. Just hold the understanding as compassion, not as a case against your parents, and let a professional help you sort old shock from present day struggle.

Chapter 7.0: How DBR Compares

Maria sat in her car outside yet another therapist's office, tired in a way that sleep did not fix. Over eight years she had tried talk therapy, then a trauma method with eye movements, then a body based approach with a lot of breathing, then something involving her nervous system and a chart of colored zones. Each one helped a little. None of it finished the job. And now someone had recommended a fourth thing, Deep Brain Reorienting, and she wanted to scream.

Her question was the reasonable one anyone would ask. How is this any different from everything I already tried? Was DBR just the old ideas in new packaging, another weekend workshop's worth of jargon, one more method that would help a little and leave her still stuck?

It is a fair question, and it deserves a fair answer, not a sales pitch. The trauma field has produced several genuinely good therapies, and they are not all the same. They tend to work on different layers of a reaction. Understanding those differences is the key to not feeling like a failure every time one approach does not fully solve things.

This chapter puts DBR next to the other trauma therapies you may have heard of, honestly, without trashing any of them. By the end you will understand what makes DBR distinct, where it overlaps with the others, and how to think about choosing, so the menu stops feeling like a trap.

By the end of this chapter you will be able to explain how Deep Brain Reorienting differs from the other main trauma therapies, in plain terms. You will see that these approaches tend to target different layers of a reaction, which is why one can succeed where another stalls. You will get a fair, respectful comparison rather than a claim that DBR beats everything. You will finish able to think clearly about which approach might fit a given person and situation, and why choosing one does not mean the others were wrong.

7.1 The Crowded Shelf

If you go looking for trauma therapy, you quickly meet a wall of names and initials. There is a lot on the shelf, and to a newcomer it can all blur together into vaguely scientific promises about healing the brain.

Here is a way to cut through the blur. Almost every trauma therapy is really making a bet about which layer of a reaction to work on. Some work on thoughts and meaning. Some work on the reprocessing of memories. Some work on body sensation. Some work on the nervous system's states of calm and alarm. They are not random. They are aimed at different floors of the same building.

Remember the sequence from earlier chapters. A trigger sets off orienting, then tension, then affect, then thoughts and meaning pile on top. That gives us a rough map, from the deepest and earliest layer up to the highest and latest. Different therapies enter that map at different points. Once you see where each one enters, the whole crowded shelf gets a lot more organized, and DBR's particular spot becomes clear.

Maria's exhaustion was not because she kept picking bad therapies. It was because each one entered the map at a different floor, and none of them had reached the specific floor where her trouble was stuck.

7.2 What Makes DBR Different

Let's place DBR on the map first. Its distinctive claim is that it enters at the earliest, deepest layer, the orienting and the shock that come before affect (Corrigan & Christie-Sands, 2020). Most therapies enter higher up, at the feeling or the thought or the memory. DBR backs all the way down to the first split second.

That is the one sentence version of the whole difference. Where does the approach enter the sequence? DBR enters at the very bottom, earlier than almost anything else, which is exactly why it can sometimes reach material that higher entering methods keep passing over.

This does not make DBR magic or superior across the board. It makes it specific. For a reaction whose root really is a locked early shock, entering at that layer can succeed where working higher up did not. For other difficulties, a higher entering approach may be the better tool. A method that reaches the basement is precious when your problem is in the basement, and unnecessary when it is on the third floor.

Keep that image as we go through the others. Everyone is working the same building. DBR just takes the stairs all the way down.

7.3 DBR And EMDR

The approach with the eye movements that many people have heard of is called **EMDR**, which stands for eye movement desensitization and reprocessing. Developed by Francine Shapiro, it helps people reprocess distressing memories, often using side to side eye movements or other rhythmic stimulation while the person holds the memory in mind (Shapiro, 2018). It is well studied and widely used, with a large research base behind it.

On our map, EMDR mostly enters at the level of the memory and its associated feelings and beliefs. It works with the disturbing memory and helps the brain file it away less painfully. That is powerful for a great many people, and it is more established in the evidence than DBR by a wide margin.

DBR enters lower, at the orienting and shock beneath the memory. Interestingly, Corrigan trained in EMDR in 1999 and worked for years as an accredited EMDR consultant before he developed DBR. DBR grew from a focus on reaching an early layer of trauma that approaches working higher up can miss (Corrigan & Christie-Sands, 2020), and it was, in a sense, his attempt to reach a layer he felt EMDR sometimes did not.

So these two are not rivals so much as neighbors working different floors. Many clinicians use both. For some people EMDR resolves things fully. For others, the ones with a stubborn early shock, DBR may reach what EMDR left behind.

7.4 Example

Meet Wei. He had done a solid course of EMDR for a specific assault, and it genuinely helped. The vivid intrusive images faded, and he could think about the event without being flooded.

The moment that lingered was subtler. Even after the images calmed, Wei still flinched hard at any unexpected touch, a reaction that predated the words of the memory. EMDR had settled the memory. This flinch sat underneath it.

What he tried first, sensibly, was more EMDR, since it had worked before. It helped less this time, because the flinch was not really about the memory content anymore. It was about the earliest shock layer, the pre affective jolt, which was a different floor than the one EMDR had cleared.

Working with a DBR trained therapist, Wei went to the flinch itself, the orienting tension before any image, and stayed with it. Over a few sessions the flinch to unexpected touch eased in a way it had not before. Neither therapy failed. They reached different layers, and he needed both.

What this means for you: One good therapy resolving part of a problem, while another part remains, does not mean either failed. Different layers sometimes need different tools.

7.5 DBR And The Body Approaches

Several respected trauma therapies work primarily with the body. **Somatic Experiencing**, developed by Peter Levine, helps people release survival energy that got trapped when a threat response could not complete (Levine, 1997). **Brainspotting**, developed by David Grand, uses points in a person's field of vision to help access and process where trauma is held (Grand, 2013). And **Polyvagal informed** work, drawing on Stephen Porges and made practical for therapy by Deb Dana, focuses on helping the nervous system move out of states of alarm or shutdown into safety and connection (Porges, 2011; Dana, 2018).

These share DNA with DBR. All of them take the body and the deep nervous system seriously, rather than working only with thoughts. If you have done any of them, you already accept the core idea that healing happens below the level of talk.

DBR's particular angle within this body oriented family is its tight focus on the specific early sequence, the orienting tension and the shock before affect, tracked in order. Where Somatic Experiencing follows the body's discharge broadly, and Polyvagal work maps nervous system states, and Brainspotting uses the visual field as an entry, DBR zeroes in on that one earliest link and works from there. Same neighborhood, different precise doorway.

None of this makes the others lesser. They are strong approaches with their own strengths and, in several cases, more research behind them. DBR is one more good tool with an unusually early point of entry.

7.6 Example

Meet Ananya. She had done Polyvagal informed work and loved it. She had learned to notice when she slid into shutdown and to gently bring herself back toward calm. It genuinely improved her daily life.

The moment it did not fully reach was the initial trigger itself. She got better at recovering after a reaction, but a particular kind of sudden criticism still launched her into shutdown just as fast as ever. She was managing the aftermath beautifully and not changing the launch.

What she had built were excellent regulation skills, which are worth a great deal. They helped her climb out of the hole. They did not fill in the hole, because the drop into it was a fast early shock her skills kicked in after.

In DBR, Ananya worked with the orienting tension at the very start of that drop, before the shutdown took hold. Meeting the launch at its root, over time, the sudden criticism began to send her down less far and less often, and her hard won regulation skills had less to clean up.

What this means for you: Skills that help you recover from a reaction and work that changes the reaction at its root are both valuable, and they are not the same thing.

7.7 Choosing Is Not Betraying

By now the big reframe should be landing. Choosing one trauma therapy does not mean the others were wrong or wasted. They tend to work different layers, so a person may genuinely need more than one over time, and the right choice depends on where their trouble actually sits.

This takes the pressure off the impossible question of which trauma therapy is best. There is no single best, any more than there is a single best tool in a toolbox. There is a best fit for a particular person, a particular problem, and a particular moment. A stubborn early shock may call for DBR. A raw, image heavy memory may call for EMDR. A nervous system stuck in alarm may call for Polyvagal informed work. Often a person benefits from a combination across their healing.

So if you have tried things that helped a little and left you stuck, you are probably not a failure and your past therapists probably were not bad. You may simply not have reached the specific layer where your trouble lives yet. That is a hopeful thought, and it is the honest one.

The practical takeaway is to stop grading the methods in the abstract and start thinking about fit. Which layer is my trouble on, and which approach enters there? That question, ideally explored with a good clinician, beats hunting for a mythical best therapy every time.

7.8 When It Doesn't Work

The most common mistake here is trying to decide which single therapy is objectively best before you have even started, as if enough research online could rank them for your situation. It cannot, and the effort usually just delays getting help.

Here is why the ranking approach fails. Fit depends on things you cannot fully know from the outside, the specific layer your trouble sits on, how your particular nervous system responds, and, hugely, the skill and the relationship you have with the actual therapist. A perfectly ranked method delivered by someone you do not click with often helps less than a decent method with a therapist you trust.

Three things to try instead of ranking in the abstract:

1. Start with the problem, not the method. Describe what stays stuck to a good clinician and let them suggest an approach that fits.

2. Weigh the relationship heavily. A therapist you feel safe with matters as much as the technique on their business card.
3. Stay open to combining or switching. If one layer clears and something remains, that is information about the next layer, not a reason to give up.

If the whole choice feels paralyzing, pick a competent, trustworthy therapist and begin. You can adjust as you learn. Starting beats optimizing.

7.9 One More Look

The trauma field has several good therapies, and they are not interchangeable. Most of them are bets about which layer of a reaction to work on, from thoughts and memories at the top down to orienting and shock at the bottom. Seeing that map organizes the crowded shelf.

DBR's distinctive spot is the very bottom, the earliest orienting and shock before affect, which is deeper than where most approaches enter. EMDR, which Corrigan trained in before creating DBR, mostly works at the level of the memory. The body approaches, Somatic Experiencing, Brainspotting, and Polyvagal informed work, share DBR's respect for the deep nervous system while entering through their own particular doorways.

None of this makes DBR superior across the board. It makes it specific, precious when the trouble is a locked early shock and unnecessary when it is not. Several of the other methods have more research behind them, which is worth remembering.

Choosing one approach does not betray the others. Fit depends on the layer, the person, and above all the therapist and the trust between you. Start with the problem, weigh the relationship, stay open to combining, and begin rather than endlessly ranking.

Chapter 8.0: Does It Actually Work

Michael was the kind of person who reads the studies. When his sister told him about Deep Brain Reorienting and how it had helped a friend of hers, his first reaction was not curiosity but caution. He had watched too many miracle treatments come and go, each with glowing stories and, underneath, almost no real evidence.

So he asked the question that a careful person should always ask. Where is the proof? Not a testimonial. Not a moving story. Actual research. Had anyone tested this properly, or was it just a charismatic idea with good marketing and a trail of hopeful anecdotes?

That question is not cynical. It is responsible, and DBR should be able to face it honestly. The worst thing a book like this could do is oversell a young method and set you up for disappointment or, worse, steer you away from treatments with stronger track records. So this chapter looks straight at the evidence, the real study that exists, what it shows, and just as importantly what it does not.

By the end you will know exactly where DBR stands scientifically, in plain terms. You will be able to hold it as what it honestly is, a promising early approach rather than a proven cure, and you will know how to talk about it without overclaiming or dismissing it.

By the end of this chapter you will understand what research has and has not shown about Deep Brain Reorienting. You will learn about the one significant study, what it found, and its real limitations. You will see the difference between a promising emerging treatment and a fully established one, and why that difference matters for your decisions. You will finish able to describe DBR's evidence honestly to a friend, a family member, or a skeptical part of yourself, without either hype or unfair dismissal.

8.1 The Fair Question

Wanting evidence is not being difficult. It is how you protect yourself from wasted time, wasted money, and false hope. Trauma treatment is a field with real science in it, and it is reasonable to ask any approach to show its work.

There is a spectrum worth understanding. At one end sit treatments with mountains of research, tested in many trials, by many independent teams, over many years. At the other end sit brand new ideas with little more than their creators' clinical impressions. Most approaches live somewhere in between, and where a method sits on that spectrum should shape how confidently you lean on it.

DBR is a young approach, so we should expect its evidence to be early rather than vast, and that is exactly what we find. The honest move is not to pretend it has more proof than it does, nor to dismiss it for being new. The honest move is to look at what actually exists and weigh it plainly.

Michael's instinct to check was the right one. Let's give his question a real answer.

8.2 The One Big Study

There is one substantial piece of research on DBR, and it is genuinely encouraging. In 2023, a team including Corrigan and the trauma researcher Ruth Lanius published a randomized controlled trial, which is the kind of study designed to give trustworthy answers (Kearney et al., 2023).

Here is what they did, in plain terms. They took 54 people who had post traumatic stress disorder and split them randomly into two groups. One group received Deep Brain Reorienting, eight sessions delivered over video. The other group waited, serving as a comparison. Then the researchers measured everyone's trauma symptoms using a standard, well respected assessment, at the start, right after treatment, and again three months later.

The results were strong. The group that received DBR showed significant reductions in their PTSD symptoms compared to the group that waited, and the improvements were still holding up three months later (Kearney et al., 2023). The size of the benefit was large by research standards, and importantly, very few people dropped out, which suggests the treatment was well tolerated even though it deals with hard material.

For a first proper study, that is a promising result. It is exactly the kind of early evidence that makes researchers want to look closer, and it is a real answer to Michael's question. Something has been tested, with reasonable rigor, and it worked.

8.3 What The Study Doesn't Prove

Now the honest other half, because a good result comes with real limits, and the researchers themselves are clear about them.

First, it was one study with a fairly small number of people. Strong findings in a small first trial need to be repeated, ideally by other independent teams, before we can be confident. Science trusts results that hold up across many studies, not a single promising one.

Second, the comparison group was a waitlist, people who simply waited. That tells us DBR beat doing nothing, which matters, but it does not tell us DBR beats other good trauma therapies. Nobody in this study was compared head to head against, say, EMDR or trauma focused talk therapy. So we cannot honestly say DBR is better than established treatments. We can only say it clearly helped more than waiting.

Third, this was described as an interim analysis, an early look at an ongoing line of research, and it came from a team closely connected to the method's creator. That is normal for a new approach, and it is also a reason to want independent replication. The researchers themselves called for larger studies, brain imaging, and direct comparisons with other therapies (Kearney et al., 2023).

None of this means DBR does not work. It means the evidence is early and promising rather than deep and settled. That is simply where a young method is.

8.4 Example

Meet Lisa. She is a careful decision maker who was considering DBR for her own trauma and wanted to choose responsibly, not emotionally.

The moment of decision came when she found conflicting messages online. Enthusiastic blog posts calling DBR revolutionary, and quieter voices noting it was new and less proven. She did not know how to weigh them.

What she tried first was looking for a simple verdict, a clear yes it works or no it does not. She could not find one, and the search left her more anxious, because the truth did not fit into a thumbs up or thumbs down.

What worked was reframing the question. Instead of is it proven, she asked is the early evidence good enough to make this a reasonable thing to try, given my situation and a skilled therapist. Seen that way, the answer became clear. One solid, encouraging study plus a coherent theory made DBR a reasonable option to explore, as long as she held realistic expectations and did not treat it as a guaranteed cure.

What this means for you: For a newer treatment, the useful question is rarely is it proven. It is closer to is the early evidence good enough to make this a sensible thing to try.

8.5 The Rest Of The Picture

Beyond that main trial, the rest of the DBR evidence is the sort you would expect for a young approach, and it is worth being clear eyed about it.

There is the underlying theory, laid out in Corrigan's writing, including the paper that first proposed the deep brain model behind DBR (Corrigan & Christie-Sands, 2020). It is important to understand what that kind of paper is. It presents a well reasoned set of hypotheses, an argument for how this might work, not proof that it does. The authors are careful to label it that way, which is to their credit.

There is also a growing collection of clinical case reports and accounts from therapists using DBR, and newer work extending it in different directions. These add real world texture and suggest the approach is spreading among practitioners. But case reports and clinical impressions, however encouraging, are a weaker form of evidence than controlled trials, because they lack the comparison that tells you the improvement was actually due to the treatment.

Put it together and you get a fair summary. One promising controlled trial, a coherent and honestly hedged theory, and a body of clinical experience that is growing. That is a real foundation for a new method. It is not yet the deep, replicated, independent evidence base that older therapies have built over decades.

8.6 Emerging Is Not Nothing

Here is the balanced place to land, and it takes a little maturity to hold. Emerging evidence is not the same as no evidence, and it is not the same as strong evidence either. DBR sits honestly in the middle, and both extremes get it wrong.

The people who call DBR revolutionary and proven are ahead of the data. The people who wave it off as unproven nonsense are ignoring a genuinely promising trial and a serious theory. The accurate view is less exciting than either and more useful. DBR is a promising, well tolerated, early stage approach with encouraging first evidence, developed by serious people, still in need of more and independent research.

That honest framing is exactly how you should talk about it, with a curious friend or a doubtful clinician alike. There is a good first study showing it helped people with PTSD more than waiting, the effects lasted a few months, and it seems gentle, but it is new, the research is early, and it has not been tested against other established therapies yet. That single, fair sentence will serve you better than any hype or any dismissal.

Holding that middle is a skill. It lets you take a young method seriously without being naive, and to stay open without being credulous. That is the posture this whole book has tried to model.

8.7 When It Doesn't Work

There are two opposite ways people misuse evidence here, and both cause trouble. The first is dismissing DBR entirely because it is not fully proven. The second is believing in it completely because of one good study or one moving story.

Here is why both go wrong. Dismissing every unproven approach would have ruled out every therapy that ever existed during its early years, including the ones now considered gold standard. And overbelieving a single study ignores how often promising first results shrink when repeated. The evidence supports neither extreme. It supports cautious openness.

Three things to try to stay balanced:

1. Match your confidence to the evidence. Let a promising early study make you curious and willing to try, not certain and evangelical.
2. Keep proven options on the table. For serious PTSD, well established treatments exist, and DBR being interesting does not mean you should skip them. A good clinician can help you weigh the options.
3. Watch the research over time. DBR is being studied further. Following how the early promise holds up is smarter than deciding once and never revisiting.

If weighing evidence feels overwhelming, that is what professionals are for. You do not have to become a research analyst. You just have to avoid the two extremes and lean on people who read this literature for a living.

8.8 The Short Answer

Asking for evidence is responsible, not cynical, and DBR can face the question honestly. There is one substantial study, a 2023 randomized controlled trial with 54 people who had PTSD, half receiving eight video sessions of DBR and half waiting. The DBR group improved significantly more, the gains lasted three months, the effect was large, and dropout was low.

That is genuinely promising for a first trial. The limits are real too. It was one smallish study, the comparison was a waitlist rather than another active therapy, it was an early analysis from a team close to the method's creator, and it needs independent replication. So DBR beat doing nothing. It has not been shown to beat established treatments.

The rest of the picture is a coherent but explicitly hypothetical theory and a growing set of clinical reports, which is the normal profile of a young approach. Emerging evidence is not nothing and it is not strong proof. DBR sits honestly in the middle.

The fair way to hold it, and to describe it, is cautious openness. Promising early evidence, gentle and well tolerated, developed by serious people, still needing more research. Match your confidence to that, keep proven options available, and watch how the science develops.

Chapter 9.0: Safety And Slowing Down

Zara had avoided trauma therapy for a decade for one reason. She was terrified that going back into the worst moments of her life would break something loose that she could not put back. She had heard stories of people who fell apart in therapy, who got worse before they got better, and she had decided she would rather stay quietly stuck than risk that.

It is a completely understandable fear, and it is not paranoid. Done badly, or too fast, trauma work really can overwhelm a person. Anyone who has been through something hard has a wise part that says, carefully, we are not doing that again without good reason. That part deserves respect, not steamrolling.

Here is what eventually let Zara try. She learned that a good trauma approach is built around not overwhelming you, that safety and pacing are not afterthoughts but the whole design. Deep Brain Reorienting, in particular, is meant to work gently, in small doses, in a way intended to keep people from being flooded.

This chapter is about that safety. How DBR is designed to go slowly, why it can be gentle even with heavy material, who it is well suited for, and, just as importantly, when it is not the right thing and what to do instead. If a cautious part of you has been reading this whole book with its arms crossed, this chapter is for that part.

By the end of this chapter you will understand how Deep Brain Reorienting is designed to avoid overwhelming people, and why it can feel gentle even though it reaches deep material. You will learn who it tends to suit, including people with complex trauma, and why even a gentle method still requires a skilled therapist. You will also learn the honest limits, when DBR is not the right first step, and when a person needs something else first. You will finish reassured about the care built into this work and clear about its boundaries.

9.1 The Fear Of Making It Worse

The fear of being made worse by therapy is common, and it comes from something real. Older and cruder ideas about trauma treatment sometimes pushed people to relive their worst experiences in full, on the theory that reliving equals healing. For some people that helped. For others it flooded them and left them shakier than before.

So if part of you resists the idea of reaching into old shock, that resistance is not weakness or avoidance. It is a protective instinct, and it is often correct that going fast and hard into trauma is a bad idea. The mistake is assuming that all trauma work means going fast and hard. It does not.

Modern, careful trauma approaches are built around the opposite principle. Go slow. Stay within what the person can handle. Keep one foot in the present at all times. DBR belongs to this careful family. Its creators specifically designed it to work with the deep brain in a way meant to reduce the risk of overwhelm rather than provoke it (Corrigan & Christie-Sands, 2020).

Zara's crossed arms were wisdom, not obstruction. The right response was not to override her caution but to show her a method that took her caution seriously.

9.2 Built To Go Gently

Recall a couple of things from earlier chapters, because they are the reasons DBR can be gentle. First, it works with small activating stimuli, slivers of a trigger, rather than asking a person to relive a whole event. Second, it anchors attention on the orienting tension, a present moment physical sensation, which keeps a person grounded in the here and now even while touching something old.

Those two features are not accidents. They are the safety design. By keeping the dose small and the anchor present, DBR tries to let a person reach the deep material without falling into it. Corrigan describes the approach as using the deep brain sequences in a way that diminishes the risk of overwhelm or of a person dissociating, meaning splitting off or going numb and checking out (Corrigan & Christie-Sands, 2020).

The research fits this picture. In the main trial, very few people dropped out, and the treatment was described as well tolerated, which is exactly what you would expect from something built to stay within a person's window of tolerance (Kearney et al., 2023). A method that regularly overwhelmed people would show high dropout. This one did not.

None of this means DBR is always comfortable. Reaching old shock can still bring up strong feeling. It means the method is structured to keep that feeling workable rather than crushing, with a skilled therapist adjusting the pace in real time.

9.3 Example

Meet Kenji. He had tried a trauma group years earlier that moved too fast for him, and he left it more anxious than he arrived. He came to DBR wary, half expecting a repeat.

The moment that reassured him came early. His DBR therapist spent the first sessions just building safety, explaining the approach, and letting Kenji set the pace, before going anywhere near the hard material.

What he had feared, based on his group experience, was being pushed to share and relive on someone else's schedule. What actually happened was the opposite. When they did begin, they worked with tiny pieces, and every time Kenji signaled he was near his limit, the therapist slowed or paused.

What worked was that the pacing stayed under his control. Because the doses were small and he never got flooded, Kenji could go further over time than he ever had in the group, precisely because he was never pushed past what he could hold.

What this means for you: A bad past experience with fast paced trauma work does not mean all trauma work will flood you. Pace and control make the difference, and good DBR keeps both.

9.4 Dissociation And Complex Trauma

For people with the heaviest histories, there is a particular concern worth naming. When trauma is severe or began very early, people often develop **dissociation**, a protective checking out where the mind goes numb, distant, or blank to escape what is too much. Dissociation is a survival skill, and it can make some trauma therapies tricky, because a person can float away from the work without anyone noticing.

DBR was developed with exactly these harder presentations in mind. Corrigan spent his career with complex, chronic, treatment resistant trauma, and much of his writing, including work on the neurobiology of dissociation, is aimed at this population (Lanius, Paulsen, & Corrigan, 2014). The gentle, anchored design is partly meant to help people stay present rather than dissociate during the work.

That said, and this matters, complex trauma and dissociation also demand more skill from the therapist, not less. Working safely with a person who dissociates requires training, experience, and careful pacing. This is one of the strongest reasons DBR is a professional method rather than a self help technique. The people it may help most are also the people for whom skilled, attuned guidance is most essential.

So the picture is balanced. DBR is designed to be suitable for hard, complex cases, which is genuinely hopeful for people who felt too complicated for other approaches. And precisely those cases call for a well trained clinician who knows how to keep the work safe.

9.5 Example

Meet Amanda. She lived with significant dissociation from early, prolonged trauma, and she had learned to disappear inside herself whenever things got intense. Past therapies had often lost her without realizing it.

The moment this showed up in DBR was when hard material approached and Amanda began to go blank and distant, her attention floating away from the room.

What made the difference was that her therapist was trained to notice the early signs of her checking out and to gently bring her back to the present anchor before she drifted too far. Instead of pressing on while Amanda was gone, the therapist paused, re grounded her, and only continued when she was truly present.

What worked was this constant, skilled attention to keeping her in the room. Because she was helped to stay present rather than dissociate, Amanda could actually process small pieces of her history for the first time, safely, at a pace her system could bear.

What this means for you: If you tend to go numb or check out under stress, you are not untreatable. You need a skilled therapist who can help you stay present, which is exactly what good DBR aims to provide.

9.6 When To Wait Or Refer

Honesty requires naming the limits. DBR is not always the right thing, and sometimes it is not the right thing yet. A responsible therapist knows this and will tell you.

If a person's life is currently in chaos or acute danger, if they are in the middle of an ongoing crisis, or if they have no stability to return to after a session, then deep trauma processing of any kind is usually not the first step. The first step is safety and stabilization, building enough steady ground to stand on before reaching into old wounds. Good clinicians assess for this and will slow down or focus elsewhere first when needed.

There is also a plain truth the DBR community states openly. Although the theory is simple, the practice can be difficult, and it does not work for everyone (Corrigan & Christie-Sands, 2020). Some people will not respond to DBR and will do better with another approach. That is not a failure of the person or the method. It is just the reality that no single therapy fits all.

And if you are in real crisis right now, or thinking about harming yourself, please treat that as more urgent than any of this. Reach out to a crisis line, an emergency service, or a trusted professional today. Deep processing work is for when you have some stable ground. Getting to safety comes first, and help is available.

9.7 When It Doesn't Work

The most important signal to respect is this. If the work itself starts to feel genuinely unsafe, if you are regularly leaving sessions flooded, destabilized, or worse rather than slowly better, something is off and it needs attention.

Here is why this matters and is not just nerves. Good DBR should keep you within what you can handle most of the time. Consistently getting overwhelmed is a sign that the pacing is wrong, the timing is wrong, or the fit between you and this therapist or this method is wrong. That is real information, not a reason to grit your teeth and push through.

Three things to try if the work feels unsafe:

1. Tell your therapist directly and immediately. A skilled clinician will slow down, add stabilization, or change the approach. How they respond also tells you a lot about them.
2. Ask about building more safety first. Sometimes the answer is not to stop but to spend more time on grounding and stability before processing.
3. Be willing to pause or change course. If the fit is wrong, finding a different therapist or a different approach is wisdom, not quitting.

Trust the protective part of you that has kept you going this far. If something feels wrong, slowing down or stepping back is always allowed. There is no prize for pushing through in trauma work, and safety is never the thing you sacrifice for progress.

9.8 The Short Answer

The fear of being made worse by trauma therapy is common and comes from something real, because older approaches sometimes pushed people to relive too much too fast. Modern, careful methods are built on the opposite principle, and DBR is one of them.

DBR is designed to be gentle by keeping doses small, working with slivers of a trigger, and anchoring attention on present moment tension so a person stays grounded rather than flooded. Corrigan built it to reduce the risk of overwhelm and dissociation, and the research showed it was well tolerated with low dropout.

It was developed with complex, dissociative, hard to treat cases in mind, which is hopeful for people who felt too complicated for other approaches. Those same cases also demand a skilled therapist, which is a core reason DBR is a professional method and not a self help technique.

It is not always the right first step. When life is in crisis, stabilization and safety come first. And DBR does not work for everyone. If the work ever feels genuinely unsafe, say so, slow down, and change course if needed. Safety is never what you trade away for progress.

Chapter 10.0: Finding The Right Help

Javier finished reading everything he could find about Deep Brain Reorienting, got genuinely hopeful, and then hit a wall. He typed find a DBR therapist near me into his phone and came up almost empty. A few names hours away. A couple offering video sessions. Nothing simple or close. His hope curdled a little into frustration. What good is a promising method if you cannot actually get to it?

This is a real problem with a new approach, and it would be dishonest to skip it. DBR is young, and the number of trained practitioners is still small compared to older, more common therapies. Finding one takes more effort than finding a general counselor, and depending on where you live, it may take creativity.

But there is good news inside the difficulty, and there are smart ways to go about the search. There is also important clarity to gain about what you can helpfully do on your own while you look, and what genuinely requires a trained professional.

This chapter is the practical one. How to find a DBR therapist, what to ask them, what to watch out for, and what to do if you cannot find one nearby. It also draws the clear line, one more time, between understanding this work and attempting it, so you know exactly what is yours to do and what is not.

By the end of this chapter you will know how to look for a trained Deep Brain Reorienting therapist and what questions to ask one before you commit. You will understand clearly what you can and cannot do on your own with this material. You will learn the warning signs of a poor fit or an overpromising practitioner. And you will have realistic options for when a DBR therapist is hard to find, so that a scarce method does not become a dead end. You will finish ready to take a concrete, sensible next step.

10.1 What You Can Do Yourself

Let's start with what is genuinely yours to do, because it is more than nothing. You can understand this material, which you now largely do. You can notice your own patterns with new eyes, seeing a recoil or a freeze as an old sequence rather than a personal flaw. You can bring more self compassion to reactions you used to judge. And you can prepare to be a good, informed participant in therapy.

You can also do the ordinary, powerful things that support any healing. Tending your sleep, your relationships, your body, and your daily stability. Building a life with enough steadiness in it that deeper work has somewhere safe to land. None of that requires special training, and all of it helps.

What you cannot safely do is perform Deep Brain Reorienting on yourself, deliberately reaching into your own old shock and trying to process it alone. I have said this throughout the book and I will say it plainly one last time. That specific work needs a trained guide, because reaching raw early shock without skilled pacing and support can bring up more than a person can hold alone, and there is no one there to help you stay grounded (Corrigan & Christie-Sands, 2020).

So the honest division is this. Understanding, self compassion, noticing, and building a stable life are yours. The deep processing work belongs in a room, virtual or real, with someone trained to do it safely.

10.2 What Needs A Professional

It is worth being specific about why the deep work needs a professional, so the rule does not feel like arbitrary gatekeeping. There are real reasons.

A trained DBR therapist does several things you cannot do for yourself. They keep the dose small and titrate the pace in real time, reading signs you might miss in yourself. They notice when you start to dissociate or get overwhelmed and bring you back. They hold the safe, steady presence that makes it possible for your deep brain to let its guard down. And they carry the training to know what to do when something unexpected surfaces.

Trying to do this alone removes every one of those protections at exactly the moment you most need them. It is a bit like the difference between reading about swimming and swimming alone in deep water for the first time. The knowledge is good and real. It is not a substitute for a competent person present while you are actually in the water.

This is not about you being incapable. It is about the nature of the work. Even DBR therapists, when they need their own trauma processed, go to another trained therapist rather than doing it on themselves. The presence of a skilled other is part of how the method works, not an optional extra.

10.3 Example

Meet Lin. After reading about DBR, she felt tempted to try working with her own old shock at home, guided by articles she had found. She was capable and independent and figured she could manage it herself.

The moment of temptation came on a hard night when an old wound felt close to the surface and she thought, maybe I can just go into this and sort it out.

What she wisely did instead was pause and ask herself what she would actually do if going into it flooded her, alone, at midnight. She had no answer, no plan, no one there. That question stopped her.

What worked was redirecting that same motivation toward finding a real therapist. She used the energy of that hard night not to dig alone but to research practitioners the next morning. A few weeks later she was doing the work safely, with someone trained to catch her if she went too far.

What this means for you: The urge to reach your own old pain is understandable, and the safest thing to do with it is to let it drive your search for the right help, not a solo attempt.

10.4 Finding A Trained Therapist

So how do you actually find one? A few approaches work better than random searching.

The most reliable route is through the official channels of the method itself. Organizations that train therapists in DBR typically maintain directories of practitioners who have completed their training. Looking for a therapist through the recognized DBR training body is the best way to be reasonably sure they are genuinely trained, rather than someone who read a little and added it to their website.

You can also ask directly. When contacting any trauma therapist, simply ask if they are trained in Deep Brain Reorienting, at what level, and how long they have been using it. A well trained clinician will answer clearly and will not be offended by the question.

Because DBR is often delivered effectively over video, as the main study showed, your search does not have to be limited to your immediate area (Kearney et al., 2023). Depending on the rules where you live, you may be able to work with a trained therapist in another city or region entirely through telehealth, which dramatically widens the pool. That single fact rescues a lot of people who have no local practitioner.

Take your time verifying training. In a newer field, it is worth making sure the person guiding you into deep work has actually been taught to do it.

10.5 Questions To Ask

Before committing to a therapist, a short set of questions saves trouble. You are allowed to interview a potential therapist. Good ones expect it.

Ask how they were trained in DBR and to what level, so you know their preparation is real. Ask how they pace the work and keep clients from being overwhelmed, which reveals how seriously they take safety. Ask how they handle it if a session gets too intense, listening for a thoughtful answer about slowing and grounding rather than pushing through. And ask about their experience with your kind of concern, since fit matters.

Pay attention not just to the answers but to how you feel talking to them. Do you feel a little safer or a little more on guard? That gut read, over a conversation or two, is real data. The relationship carries a great deal of the healing, so a therapist you sense you can trust is worth as much as an impressive list of trainings.

You are hiring someone for delicate, important work. It is completely appropriate to choose carefully.

10.6 Example

Meet Carlos. He found two DBR trained therapists in his region and was not sure how to choose between them, since both looked qualified on paper.

The moment of clarity came in the initial phone consultations. Both were competent. But one rushed him a little and seemed eager to book sessions, while the other slowed down, answered his questions patiently, and asked how he was feeling about starting.

What Carlos had assumed was that credentials would decide it. On paper the choice was a toss up. What actually decided it was the felt sense of safety in those first conversations.

What worked was trusting that difference. He chose the therapist he felt calmer with, and that sense of safety turned out to be the foundation that let the deeper work go well.

What this means for you: When two therapists look equally qualified, let how safe you feel with each one break the tie. That feeling is not a minor detail. It is central to the work.

10.7 When You Can't Find One

Sometimes, despite real effort, there is simply no DBR therapist you can reach, even by video. This is a genuine possibility with a young method, and it is not the end of the road.

Here is why it is not a dead end. As earlier chapters showed, DBR is one member of a family of deep, body oriented trauma therapies, several of which are more widely available and have strong track records of their own. If you cannot access DBR, a skilled therapist trained in Somatic Experiencing, Brainspotting, EMDR, or sensorimotor and Polyvagal informed work may reach much of the same territory (Levine, 1997; Ogden, Minton, & Pain, 2006; van der Kolk, 2014). The goal is healing, not a particular brand.

Three things to try if DBR is out of reach:

1. Widen your search by video across your whole region or country, within the rules that apply where you live. Telehealth solves this for many people.
2. Get on a waitlist while starting something else. You can begin with an available, related approach now and switch to DBR later if a practitioner opens up.

3. Ask a trusted trauma therapist for guidance. Even one not trained in DBR can often help you find good care and may know who nearby is.

If access is hard right now, that is frustrating and it is not a verdict on your worth or your prospects. Good trauma care comes in more than one form, and the understanding you have gained will make you a better participant in any of them.

10.8 When It Doesn't Work

The warning sign to take seriously here is a practitioner who overpromises or who pressures you. Anyone guaranteeing a cure, promising to fix you in a set number of sessions, or pushing you to go faster than you are comfortable is showing you something important about themselves.

Here is why this matters. DBR is a young, gentle, honestly hedged approach, and a good practitioner reflects that honesty. Grand promises and pressure run against the spirit of the method and against good trauma care in general. A clinician overselling DBR either misunderstands it or is not being straight with you.

Three things to try if a practitioner feels off:

1. Notice guarantees and pressure as red flags. Honest trauma work does not come with a money back miracle attached.
2. Give yourself full permission to leave. You are never obligated to continue with someone who does not feel right, even a few sessions in.
3. Return to the questions from earlier in this chapter. A trustworthy therapist answers them openly. Evasion or irritation is telling.

Finding the right person can take a couple of tries, and that is normal, not a sign that help will not work for you. The search is worth doing carefully, because the right fit is a large part of why this work succeeds.

10.9 Wrapping Up

What is yours to do on your own is real. Understanding the material, seeing your patterns with kinder and clearer eyes, building a stable supportive life, and preparing to be a good participant in therapy. What is not yours to do alone is the deep processing of old shock, which needs a trained guide to keep it safe.

To find that guide, look through the recognized DBR training organizations and their directories, ask any trauma therapist directly about their DBR training and level, and remember that video sessions can widen your search well beyond your local area. Interview potential therapists, ask how they pace and keep the work safe, and weigh how safe you feel with them as heavily as their credentials.

If you cannot find a DBR therapist even by video, that is not a dead end. Related deep, body oriented trauma therapies are more widely available and can reach much of the same ground, and you can start with one now and switch later. Watch out for anyone who overpromises or pressures you, and give yourself permission to choose carefully and to leave a poor fit.

Chapter 11.0: If You Are A Therapist

Gemma, the counselor you met back in the first chapter, finally understood DBR well enough to make a decision. And she found herself standing at a familiar crossroads that a lot of good therapists reach. She was intrigued. She could see how this might reach the clients who had plateaued on her. And she was tired, and cautious about pouring another chunk of time and money into another training that might or might not earn its place in her work.

If you are a therapist reading this, that crossroads may be yours too. You have gotten the plain language tour along with everyone else, and now you have a more specific question than a general reader does. Not just what is DBR, but should I actually train in this, and what would that involve.

This chapter is written for you. It lays out who can train, how the training tends to be structured, what it costs in time and money, and how DBR might fit alongside the tools you already use. It also holds the ethical line clearly, because you, more than any other reader, need to know exactly where understanding ends and trained practice begins.

You are welcome to read this even if you are not a clinician. It will show you what the professional path looks like from the inside. But it is aimed at the therapist trying to decide.

By the end of this chapter you, as a clinician, will understand the DBR training pathway well enough to make an informed decision about pursuing it. You will know the typical prerequisites, how the training is usually structured, and roughly what it asks of you in time and money. You will understand how DBR tends to fit alongside other modalities rather than replacing them, and where the ethical boundaries of competence sit. You will finish able to decide, with clear eyes, if training in DBR is right for you and your practice right now.

11.1 Why Therapists Are Curious

The pull toward DBR, for most clinicians, comes from a specific and honorable place. It is the stuck client. Nearly every experienced trauma therapist carries a small number of people who have done everything right and still have not fully healed, and those cases sit heavily.

DBR speaks directly to that ache. Its whole premise is that there is an early layer, the shock before affect, that other methods often pass over, and that reaching it can help exactly the people who plateaued elsewhere (Corrigan & Christie-Sands, 2020). For a therapist who has watched a good client stall, that premise is hard to ignore. It offers a possible answer to the question that keeps you up, why did this person not get all the way better.

There is also the appeal of the approach itself. Many clinicians drawn to DBR already work in body based or brain based ways and find its careful, deep focus a natural extension of what they value. It fits the sensibility of therapists who trust the nervous system and distrust purely top down talk.

Gemma's curiosity was really about her plateaued clients. That is usually the honest engine underneath a therapist's interest, and it is a good reason to look closely, as long as the looking stays clear eyed about cost and evidence.

11.2 Who Can Train

DBR training is designed for clinicians, not for the general public, and there are real prerequisites. Understanding them helps you know if you are eligible and why the bar is set where it is.

Training is generally open to licensed or otherwise qualified mental health professionals, and it typically expects a minimum level of experience, commonly around two years of post qualification practice, along with a background working with trauma and early adversity (Corrigan & Christie-Sands, 2020). In other words, this is continuing education for established trauma clinicians, not an entry level certificate.

The reasons for these requirements connect to everything in this book. DBR reaches raw, deep material, often in complex and dissociative clients. Working there safely assumes you already have solid clinical foundations, trauma knowledge, and the judgment that comes from experience. The prerequisites are there to make sure practitioners can hold what the method surfaces.

If you meet those criteria, you are likely eligible. If you are newer to the field, the honest guidance is to build your general trauma competence first. DBR will still be there when you have the grounding it assumes, and you will practice it better for having waited.

11.3 Example

Meet James. He is a clinical social worker with three years of trauma experience who felt ready to add a deeper modality and was drawn to DBR.

The moment of decision came when he checked the prerequisites and found he met them, with his license and his trauma background in place.

What he had worried about was if he was experienced enough to work at the depth DBR reaches. It was a fair worry, and he took it seriously rather than brushing it aside.

What worked was that he had genuinely built the foundations the training assumes, solid trauma knowledge and a few years of real cases, so entering DBR training was a reasonable next step rather than a leap past his competence. He trained, practiced carefully, and integrated it gradually.

What this means for you: If you meet the prerequisites and, more importantly, actually have the clinical grounding behind them, DBR training can be a sound next step rather than an overreach.

11.4 How The Training Works

DBR training is usually structured in sequential levels that build on one another, rather than a single weekend workshop. You generally start at the first level and progress, with each stage assuming the last.

The early level tends to focus on the core of the method, working with shock at the root of traumatic experience. A later level typically turns to attachment shock and attachment wounding, the relational material from Chapter 6, and the deep seeking of connection (Corrigan & Christie-Sands, 2020). The progression mirrors the logic of the approach itself, foundational shock first, then the more layered attachment material.

The format is experiential, not just lectures. Trainings generally combine teaching with live demonstrations, small group practice sessions where you work the method with peers under guidance, and question and answer time, often with encouragement to practice between trainings and sometimes with ongoing consultation. This hands on, supervised structure is essential, because a method like this cannot be learned from slides alone. You have to feel it and practice it with feedback.

Because it is sequential and practice based, becoming competent in DBR is a process over time, not a one weekend credential. That is a feature. Depth takes staged learning, and the structure reflects respect for how much skill safe deep work requires.

11.5 The Investment

Time and money matter in any continuing education decision, so here is the honest picture, with a clear caveat that exact figures change and you should verify current details directly with training providers.

Each level of DBR training carries its own fee, and as a rough sense of scale, per level costs have tended to fall in the range of several hundred dollars, with some variation for membership status, location, and the specific provider. Since there are multiple sequential levels, the full pathway represents a real cumulative investment of both money and time, spread across the stages rather than paid all at once. Trainings have been offered in various countries and increasingly online, which affects both cost and access.

Because these details shift, treat any specific number you see, including secondhand ones, as a starting point to confirm rather than a fixed fact. Pricing, level structure, and availability are exactly the kind of thing that changes year to year, so go to the current source before you budget.

The larger point for your decision is that DBR is a meaningful investment, not a casual add on. That is precisely why understanding it well first, which you now do, is so valuable. You are in a position to decide if that investment fits your practice and your finances, rather than committing blind and hoping.

11.6 Example

Meet Raj. He is a seasoned psychologist who was interested in DBR but decided, after honest reflection, that this was not the right year to train.

The moment of clarity came when he looked at his actual calendar and budget and saw that he was already stretched thin, mid way through another certification and carrying a heavy caseload.

What he had felt was a pull to jump in now, driven partly by fear of missing out on a method everyone was discussing. That urgency was real but not wise.

What worked was giving himself permission to wait. He decided to finish his current training, steady his schedule, and revisit DBR the following year from a place of capacity rather than overwhelm. The method was not going anywhere, and he would learn it better rested.

What this means for you: Deciding not to train right now can be the mature choice. A method worth learning is worth learning when you actually have the capacity to learn it well.

11.7 Fitting DBR Into Your Practice

If you do train, it helps to understand how DBR tends to live alongside your existing tools, because it is generally an addition rather than a replacement. Corrigan and others position it as complementing other approaches, and many DBR clinicians continue to use EMDR, parts work, somatic methods, and more, choosing DBR when a case calls for reaching that early shock layer (Corrigan & Christie-Sands, 2020).

There is also an ethical boundary to hold firmly, and as a clinician you know this territory. Until you are actually trained, you should not be practicing DBR, only, at most, letting your understanding of the shock layer inform how you think and pace within the modalities you are already qualified in. Reading this book, or any book, does not make you a DBR practitioner. That distinction is about scope of competence, and it protects both you and your clients.

Even the language matters. Being DBR informed in your thinking is not the same as offering DBR, and it is worth being honest with clients and yourself about which one you are actually doing. The trademarked method delivered with training is a different thing from a general sensitivity to early orienting and shock.

Held that way, DBR can become one more considered option in a thoughtful practice, reached for when the case fits, integrated with respect for what your other tools do well.

11.8 When It Doesn't Work

The most common misstep for clinicians here is training in DBR and expecting it to transform every stuck case, or expecting to feel competent immediately after a first workshop. Both set you up for disappointment.

Here is why. DBR is one tool with a specific strength, not a master key, and like any depth method it takes real practice before it feels natural in the room. Corrigan's own community is candid that the practice is difficult and does not work for everyone, which applies to your learning curve as much as to client outcomes (Corrigan & Christie-Sands, 2020). Early clumsiness is normal, and not every client will respond.

Three things to try if your DBR practice disappoints early:

1. Expect a learning curve and seek consultation. Depth methods feel awkward before they feel fluent. Ongoing supervision or peer consultation shortens the gap.
2. Hold realistic outcome expectations. Judge DBR as a useful option for the right cases, not as a cure for your whole caseload.
3. Keep your other tools active. DBR joins your kit rather than replacing it, so keep offering what already serves your clients well.

If, after fair effort, DBR does not fit how you work or who you serve, that is legitimate information. Not every good method suits every good clinician, and choosing not to carry it forward is a respectable decision, not a failure.

11.9 The Main Ideas

Therapists are drawn to DBR mainly by the stuck client, the person who did everything right and still did not fully heal, since DBR aims at an early shock layer other methods often miss. That is an honest reason to look closely, held alongside clear eyes about evidence and cost.

Training is continuing education for established trauma clinicians, typically expecting a license, a couple of years of experience, and a trauma background, because the method reaches deep material that assumes solid foundations. It is structured in sequential, experiential levels, foundational shock first and attachment shock later, combining teaching, demonstrations, supervised practice, and consultation over time rather than in one weekend.

It is a real investment of money and time across multiple levels, and exact figures change, so verify current details directly rather than trusting any secondhand number. Understanding DBR well first, as you now do, lets you make that investment decision with clear eyes.

If you train, DBR generally complements your existing tools rather than replacing them, reached for when a case calls for the early shock layer. And until trained, you are not practicing DBR, only letting an understanding of it inform work you are already qualified to do. That scope boundary protects you and your clients both.

Chapter 12.0: Reading More On Your Own

Ming closed this book, or one like it, and felt something she had not felt about the topic before. Ready for more. The plain language version had done its job. She understood DBR now, and instead of feeling finished, she felt curious to go deeper, to read the real sources, to hear the ideas from the people who built them.

Then she looked at the main academic book on Deep Brain Reorienting, the serious one, and felt that old flicker of intimidation return. It was thick. It was written for specialists. It was the very door that had felt locked before she found a gentle way in.

Here is the good news. You are not the same reader who would have bounced off that book at the start. You now have the map, the vocabulary, and the core ideas. That changes everything about how the harder sources will land. Words that would have stopped you cold now have meaning attached to them, because you met them here first, in plain form.

This chapter is your guide to going further, if you want to. What the main book is and how to approach it without drowning. What the key research papers are and how to make sense of them. And how to build a sensible plan for learning more, at your own pace, that ends where all of this should end, in a conversation with a real professional rather than a solo research project.

By the end of this chapter you will know exactly where to go if you want to learn more about Deep Brain Reorienting, and how to approach those sources without getting lost. You will understand what the main academic book offers and how to read it selectively. You will know the key research papers and what each one is for. You will have a simple plan for deepening your knowledge at your own pace. And you will keep in view that reading more is preparation for getting help, not a substitute for it.

12.1 So You Want To Go Deeper

First, permission. You do not have to read anything more. If this book gave you what you came for, a solid understanding and a clear next step, you are done, and that is a complete and good outcome. Going deeper is for the curious, not a requirement for anyone.

But if you are curious, that curiosity is worth honoring. Some people want the fuller picture, the actual studies, the theory in the creators' own words. Reading more can deepen your understanding, sharpen your questions for a therapist, and satisfy the honest hunger to really get it.

The trick is to go deeper without falling into the trap that stops so many people, which is opening the hardest source first, getting overwhelmed, and concluding they are not smart enough for the topic. You already avoided that trap once by starting here. The same principle applies going forward. Move from easier to harder, with your existing understanding as the bridge.

Ming's readiness was real, and so was her intimidation. Both can be true. The way through is to approach the harder material strategically rather than bravely charging at the thickest book and hoping.

12.2 The Main Book

The central text is *Deep Brain Reorienting: Understanding the Neuroscience of Trauma, Attachment Wounding, and DBR Psychotherapy*, by Frank Corrigan along with Hannah Young and Jessica Christie-Sands (Corrigan et al., 2024). This is the definitive account, written by the method's creator and close colleagues. If you read one deeper source, this is it.

It helps to know how it is built. Broadly, the book moves from the theory, the deep brain science and the model of how trauma and attachment wounding work, into the clinical practice, how DBR is actually done. That structure is useful, because it means you can choose your entry point. If you care most about the ideas, the earlier, theoretical portion is your target. If you care most about what the therapy looks like in practice, the later, clinical portion may serve you better.

You do not have to read it front to back, and you do not have to finish it. Readers of the book, including clinicians, have noted that the brainstem science gets dense and that the authors themselves are honest about parts of the model being hypothetical. So give yourself permission to read selectively, to skim the densest science if it is not your aim, and to take what is useful without mastering every page.

Approached that way, with your plain language grounding already in place, the main book becomes a rich resource rather than a locked door. You are reading it to deepen a picture you already hold, not to build the picture from scratch, and that makes all the difference.

12.3 Example

Meet Akira. He wanted to read the main DBR book but had bounced off dense academic texts before and worried this would be another abandoned purchase.

The moment of doubt came when the first heavy pages of brain science slowed him down, just as he had feared.

What he had planned to do was read it cover to cover in order, treating every page as required, which is exactly what had defeated him with hard books in the past.

What worked was changing his strategy. He gave himself permission to skim the densest science, to focus on the sections about how the therapy actually works, and to stop when he had what he wanted. Freed from the duty to master all of it, he actually finished the parts that mattered to him and came away genuinely more informed.

What this means for you: You are allowed to read a hard book selectively. Taking the parts that serve you and skimming the rest is not cheating. It is how busy, sensible people learn.

12.4 The Key Papers

Beyond the book, two research papers are worth knowing about, because they are the primary sources behind everything in this book, and you can often find at least their summaries freely online.

The first is the 2020 paper by Corrigan and Christie-Sands that laid out the deep brain theory behind DBR, published in a journal called *Medical Hypotheses* (Corrigan & Christie-Sands, 2020). Remember what kind of paper this is. As its journal name signals, it presents a hypothesis, a well reasoned proposal for how this works, rather than proof. It is the theoretical foundation, valuable for understanding the ideas, not evidence of results.

The second is the 2023 randomized controlled trial, the study we walked through in the evidence chapter, published in the *European Journal of Psychotraumatology* (Kearney et al., 2023). This is the results paper, the one that tested DBR on people with PTSD and found encouraging early evidence. If you want to see the actual research rather than descriptions of it, this is the one to look up.

You do not need to read these in full, and the technical language can be heavy. But even reading their abstracts, the short summaries at the top, will give you the core of each straight from the source. Knowing these two papers exist, and what each is for, one theory and one evidence, is often enough.

12.5 Building A Learning Plan

If you want to keep learning, a simple sequence keeps you from getting lost. Think of it as moving outward in rings, from what you already have toward the primary sources and then toward a real conversation.

Start where you are, with the solid understanding this book gave you. From there, if you want the ideas in more depth, read selectively in the main book, choosing the theoretical or clinical portions based on your interest. If you want the evidence, look up the abstract of the 2023 trial. Along the way, talks and interviews with DBR clinicians, which appear from time to time in podcasts and professional recordings, can be a gentler way to absorb more than dense text allows.

Then, crucially, let the whole plan point toward a person. The natural endpoint of learning about DBR is not becoming a self taught expert. It is being well prepared to talk with a trained therapist, ask good questions, and make an informed choice about your own care or your own practice. Reading is the on ramp. A real professional relationship is the road.

Set the pace yourself. There is no deadline and no test. A little reading, digested slowly, with your understanding growing in rings, beats a heroic push that burns you out on page forty.

12.6 When It Doesn't Work

The most common way going deeper backfires is getting lost in the dense material, feeling stupid, and concluding you do not really understand DBR after all. That conclusion is false and worth heading off.

Here is why it happens. Academic writing is often hard to read on purpose, packed with technical language for a specialist audience. Struggling with it says nothing about your intelligence or your grasp of the ideas. Plenty of smart people, including trained clinicians, find these sources heavy going. The difficulty is in the writing, not in you.

Three things to try if the deeper reading defeats you:

1. Drop back to summaries. Abstracts, plain language articles, and recorded talks carry the core ideas without the dense prose. There is no shame in the easier version.
2. Read for the gist, not every detail. You do not need to follow every technical argument to understand the main points. Let the small stuff wash past.
3. Remember you already understand the essentials. This book gave you the real core. The harder sources add depth, not a secret you are missing.

If the academic material simply is not for you, that is completely fine. You can understand DBR well, choose good care, and never read a research paper in your life. The deeper reading is a bonus for the curious, not a hurdle you must clear.

12.7 One More Look

If you want to learn more, honor that curiosity, and go about it strategically rather than by charging at the hardest source first. Your plain language grounding is the bridge that makes the deeper material readable now in a way it would not have been before.

The central text is Corrigan, Young, and Christie-Sands's book, which moves from deep brain theory into clinical practice. Read it selectively, choosing the theoretical or the clinical portions by your interest, skimming the densest science, and giving yourself full permission not to finish it. Two papers sit behind everything here, the 2020 theory paper in Medical Hypotheses and the 2023 trial in the European Journal of Psychotraumatology, and even their abstracts carry the core.

Build a learning plan that moves outward in rings, from what you know, to selective reading, to talks and interviews, and finally toward a real conversation with a trained professional, which is where all of this is meant to lead. Set your own pace, since there is no deadline and no test.

And if the dense material defeats you, that reflects the writing, not your intelligence or your understanding. Drop to summaries, read for the gist, and rest assured you already hold the essentials.

Chapter 13.0: Where You Are Now

Remember Elena from the very first chapter, sitting in her car in the office parking lot, asking what was wrong with her because a coworker's throat clearing could still send her somewhere small and afraid. See her now, months later, in that same car, but different. She has read her way into understanding. She knows the reaction that ambushes her is not a flaw in her character. It is an old, fast sequence in the deep part of her brain, and it can be reached.

She has not been magically cured. That is not what this is. But something has shifted that matters just as much at this stage. She is no longer confused and ashamed. She knows what she is dealing with, she knows it has a name and a logic, and she knows there is a kind of help built to reach exactly the layer where she is stuck. She has an appointment next week with a trained therapist. She feels, for the first time in a long time, oriented.

That word is a fitting place to end, because orienting is where this whole approach begins. You have spent this book learning how the brain turns toward what matters. Along the way, you have turned toward something too. A clearer understanding of a promising approach, and a sense of where you stand in relation to it.

This final chapter is short. It gathers what you now know, helps you choose your own next step, and sends you off with one last piece of honesty. You came in curious and maybe a little intimidated. Look at where you are now.

By the end of this short closing chapter you will have a clear summary of everything you learned, gathered in one place. You will have a simple way to choose your own next step, whatever your situation. And you will carry away a final, honest framing of Deep Brain Reorienting that holds both real hope and clear eyed realism, so you leave neither oversold nor cynical, but genuinely informed and ready to act as you see fit.

13.1 Look How Far You Came

Think back to before you opened this book. Deep Brain Reorienting was probably just a set of intimidating words, a thing you had heard about and could not really explain. The one real book on it looked like a locked door. You were curious and unsure if you would understand.

Now look at what you can do. You can explain, in plain language, what DBR is and the idea it rests on, the shock before feeling. You can name the deep brain players and what they do. You can picture a session. You can compare DBR fairly to other trauma therapies. You can describe its evidence honestly, neither overselling nor dismissing. You can speak to its safety and its limits. That is a real understanding, and you built it one small step at a time.

This is worth pausing on, because beginners rarely give themselves credit. You took something that stops most people at the door and you walked all the way through it. Not by being a specialist, but by being willing to go slowly and let it build. That same patient willingness is exactly what serves people well in healing itself.

Whatever you do next, you do it as someone who understands. That alone puts you ahead of where you started, and ahead of most people who have heard the term.

It also changes how you will hear the topic from here on. The next time DBR comes up in a podcast, an article, or a conversation, you will not feel the small sting of being on the outside of something everyone else seems to grasp. You will know what they mean, and often more than they do. You will be able to tell the careful descriptions from the breathless ones. That quiet confidence, the settledness of actually understanding a thing that used to intimidate you, is worth more than it sounds, and it is yours to keep.

13.2 What You Know Now

Let's gather the core of it in one place, so you carry it cleanly. DBR is a trauma therapy that works with the oldest, deepest part of the brain, the part that reacts to threat in the first split second, before emotion forms. Its central idea is the shock before feeling, and its central move is returning gently to that early moment and letting the deep brain complete a sequence that got locked.

It works with orienting tension, small physical tension in the face, head, and neck, using tiny doses of a trigger so a person is not flooded. A session is quiet and slow. It reaches an early layer that many therapies pass over, which is why it can sometimes help people who stayed stuck elsewhere, including those with attachment wounds and no dramatic event to point to. Its evidence is early and promising, one encouraging trial and a serious theory, rather than deep and settled. It is designed to be gentle, it suits complex cases, and it always requires a trained therapist. It is not a cure all, and it does not work for everyone.

That paragraph is the whole book in miniature. If you forget everything else, keep that.

13.3 Elena's Next Step

Return to Elena one last time, because her next step models the point of all this. She did not become her own therapist. She did not try to fix her deepest reactions alone with what she read. And she did not let the newness of DBR either dazzle her into blind faith or scare her off entirely.

The moment that mattered was quiet. She simply used what she now understood to make one good decision, booking a session with a trained DBR therapist she had carefully checked, going in with realistic hope rather than a demand for a miracle.

What she had done wrong for years was suffer in confusion, assuming she was broken, not knowing there was a name or a map or a kind of help aimed at her exact stuckness.

What worked was letting understanding become action. The knowledge did not heal her by itself. It pointed her, clearly and calmly, toward the help that might. Understanding was the compass. The therapist is the road.

What this means for you: The purpose of everything you learned is not to know more. It is to help you take one good, informed next step, whatever that step is for you.

13.4 Choosing Your Next Step

Your own next step depends on where you stand, and any of several are right. If something in this book spoke to your own stuckness, your step might be to look for a trained therapist, using the guidance from the chapter on finding help. If you are curious but not ready, your step might simply be to sit with what you learned and let it settle, which is completely legitimate.

If you are a therapist, your step might be to weigh the training honestly against your capacity and finances, deciding to pursue it, to wait, or to let an understanding of the shock layer quietly inform work you already do well. If you love someone who is stuck, your step might be to share what you now understand, gently, so they know an option exists. And if you simply came for understanding and got it, your step might be to close the book satisfied. That is a real ending too.

Whatever your step, let it be small enough that you can actually take it. That has been a quiet theme running under this whole book. The reactions DBR works with are small at their root, a flinch, a tightening, a split second turn. The way in is small too, a sliver of a trigger rather than the whole flood. And your next move can be small in the same way. One phone call to ask a therapist about their training. One evening rereading the chapter that spoke to you most. One honest conversation with someone you trust about what you are considering. Small steps are not lesser steps. They are the ones that actually get taken, and a step you can complete beats a grand plan you never start.

There is no single correct next step, and there is no deadline. Hold your hope loosely and let it coexist with patience. DBR is promising, not proven, so a reasonable step is a considered one, not a leap. If the wise, cautious part of you wants to move slowly, let it. That caution has carried you this far, and it will not steer you wrong now. Whatever you choose, choose it as the informed person you have become over these pages.

13.5 A Last Honesty

One final piece of straight talk, because this book has tried to earn your trust by being honest, and it will not stop now. Deep Brain Reorienting is genuinely exciting, and it is genuinely early. Both are true, and holding both is the mature place to stand.

The excitement is real. Here is an approach reaching for a layer of trauma that older methods often miss, with a coherent theory and an encouraging first trial, offering possible help to people who felt beyond help. That is worth being hopeful about. The earliness is real too. One study, a hypothesis level theory, a small community of practitioners, and open questions still to be answered. That is worth being measured about.

So do not leave this book either oversold or cynical. Leave it clear. DBR might be part of the answer for you or someone you love, and it might not, and the honest way to find out is to approach it with open, patient, informed hope, ideally alongside a skilled professional. That posture, curious but grounded, is the one that serves you in this and in almost everything.

You came in a beginner. You are leaving as someone who understands, who can tell hope from hype, and who knows how to take a good next step. That is exactly what this book set out to give you.

13.6 The Last Word

You started with a set of intimidating words and a locked door. You are ending with a real, plain language understanding of Deep Brain Reorienting, from the shock before feeling to the deep brain players to the session, the comparisons, the evidence, the safety, and the path to help.

The heart of it fits in a breath. DBR reaches the earliest layer of a trauma reaction, the shock before the feeling, and gently helps the deep brain finish what it once could not. It is promising and early, gentle and serious, and it always calls for a trained guide.

The purpose of all this understanding is not knowledge for its own sake. It is one good next step, and which step is right depends entirely on you. Look for help, sit with it, train in it, share it, or simply close the book content. Each is a fine ending.

Hold your hope loosely and your curiosity warmly. Whatever comes next, you go into it oriented, which, fittingly, is exactly where this whole approach begins.

References

Corrigan, F. M., & Christie-Sands, J. (2020). An innate brainstem self-other system involving orienting, affective responding, and polyvalent relational seeking: Some clinical implications for a "Deep Brain Reorienting" trauma psychotherapy approach. *Medical Hypotheses, 136*, 109502. https://doi.org/10.1016/j.mehy.2019.109502

Corrigan, F. M., Young, H., & Christie-Sands, J. (2024). *Deep brain reorienting: Understanding the neuroscience of trauma, attachment wounding, and DBR psychotherapy.* Routledge.

Dana, D. (2018). *The polyvagal theory in therapy: Engaging the rhythm of regulation.* W. W. Norton.

Grand, D. (2013). *Brainspotting: The revolutionary new therapy for rapid and effective change.* Sounds True.

Kearney, B. E., Corrigan, F. M., Frewen, P. A., Nevill, S., Harricharan, S., Andrews, K., Jetly, R., McKinnon, M. C., & Lanius, R. A. (2023). A randomized controlled trial of Deep Brain Reorienting: A neuroscientifically guided treatment for post-traumatic stress disorder. *European Journal of Psychotraumatology, 14*(2), 2240691. https://doi.org/10.1080/20008066.2023.2240691

Lanius, U. F., Paulsen, S. L., & Corrigan, F. M. (Eds.). (2014). *Neurobiology and treatment of traumatic dissociation: Toward an embodied self.* Springer Publishing Company.

Levine, P. A. (1997). *Waking the tiger: Healing trauma.* North Atlantic Books.

Ogden, P., Minton, K., & Pain, C. (2006). *Trauma and the body: A sensorimotor approach to psychotherapy.* W. W. Norton.

Panksepp, J. (1998). *Affective neuroscience: The foundations of human and animal emotions.* Oxford University Press.

Porges, S. W. (2011). *The polyvagal theory: Neurophysiological foundations of emotions, attachment, communication, and self-regulation.* W. W. Norton.

Shapiro, F. (2018). *Eye movement desensitization and reprocessing (EMDR) therapy: Basic principles, protocols, and procedures* (3rd ed.). Guilford Press.

Siegel, D. J. (2012). *The developing mind: How relationships and the brain interact to shape who we are* (2nd ed.). Guilford Press.

van der Kolk, B. A. (2014). *The body keeps the score: Brain, mind, and body in the healing of trauma.* Viking.

www.ingramcontent.com/pod-product-compliance
Lightning Source LLC
LaVergne TN
LVHW022110200926
848481LV00003B/1136
* 9 7 9 8 9 0 5 9 9 8 5 1 5 *